THE OLD TESTAMENT
EXPRESS

by
Terry Hall

VICTOR
BOOKS a division of SP Publications, Inc.
WHEATON. ILLINOIS 60187

Offices also in
Whitby, Ontario, Canada
Amersham-on-the-Hill, Bucks, England

This book is designed to help you understand the Old Testament and discover how it applies to your life today. You can read it by yourself or study it with the help of a group. Student activity booklets (Rip-Off Sheets) and a leader's guide with visual aids (SonPower Multi-use Transparency Masters) are available from your local Christian bookstore or from the publisher.

A one-day seminar based on the material presented in *The Old Testament Express* is also available. For more information on how your church or organization can sponsor a Bible Panorama Seminar, contact the author at Media Ministries, 516 East Wakeman, Wheaton, IL 60187 (312/665-4594).

Library of Congress Catalog Card Number: 84-52042
ISBN: 0-88207-599-3

Recommended Dewey Decimal Classification: 248.83
Suggested Subject Heading: YOUTH—RELIGIOUS LIFE

CONTENTS

CONTENTS

to
JOHN GEBHARDT
a special nephew
and
friend

1

THE BIBLE PUZZLE

Have you ever tried to assemble a jigsaw puzzle without seeing the completed picture on the box lid? Or traveled to an unfamiliar destination without directions or a map? Or listened to a teacher rattle off seemingly useless details because he didn't give you an outline?

Many things in life make more sense when we are able to see "the big picture." The Bible is no exception. To many people, the Bible is like a gigantic jigsaw puzzle with a lost box top—just *lots* of pieces picked up from Sunday School, sermons, and Scripture reading. But if all those pieces aren't somehow tied together, the Bible can seem incredibly complex. (As late as the ninth grade, I thought the Old Testament was for old Christians, and the New Testament was for new ones!)

This book is designed to help you interlock the individual puzzle pieces you have collected from the Old Testament and see the big picture. Such a study has many benefits. Among other things, you will:

- [ ] Feel more "at home" in the Old Testament's library of 39 books and 929 chapters
- [ ] Grasp the *major* messages of the Old Testament
- [ ] Relate God's Word from "way back then" to your world today
- [ ] Condense the Bible's topics to three key words
- [ ] Discover how all Scripture relates to Jesus Christ
- [ ] Draw a map that will summarize the Bible's major points
- [ ] Summarize the theme of each Old Testament book in three words

Beginning with the Basics

Here are some easy ways to remember how the Bible is put together.

"The Bible" is two words, reminding us of its two big parts: Old Testament and New Testament. The word "testament" simply means a will. The Bible reveals God's will for us in an older part and a newer part.

Count the letters in the words "Old" (3) and "Testament" (9). Put these two figures side-by-side to remember there are 39 books in the Old Testament. Add them together to recall how many Hebrew tribes there were (12).

The words "New" and "Testament" also have 3 and 9 letters. Multiply these two numbers to get the 27 books of the New Testament. Add them together to recall how many apostles Jesus appointed, through whom He could expand His ministry (12).

Subtracting the 3 from the 9 for each Testament

results in two 6s, which side-by-side equal the total number of books in the Bible (66).

The Big Three

The word "HEP" forms an acrostic that will help you mentally march through the three main subjects of the entire Bible:

History (Past)
Experience (Present)
Prophecy (Future)

Each Testament begins with a section of *history* giving an account of how God *has* already worked in His world through the people He created. History is really "His story." These sections contain the "action-advancing" books which provide us with the "story line" of the Bible.

After the history books in each Testament, you will find the *experience* books. They deal more with how God wants to work in our lives *now,* and describe the hopes and dreams of individuals who desire a closer walk with their God.

Both Testaments end with a section of *prophecy,* largely a record of things God *will* do in the future. The prophecy books are full of expectation and anticipation.

The Bible, then, is about what God has done, is doing, and will yet do. Divide 66 (Bible books) by 3 (Bible topics) to remember there are 22 Bible history books. So to read the big story of the Bible, you only need to read one third of its books! If you read the first 17 of the Old Testament and the first 5 of the New Testament, you will cover the whole story line of the Bible in terms of plot and action.

Don't look for a story line to continue in the Old Testament after the Book of Esther. Rather, think of

THE TOPICAL BIBLE

HISTORY	EXPERIENCE	PROPHECY
Genesis	Job	Isaiah
Exodus	Psalms	Jeremiah
Leviticus	Proverbs	Lamentations
Numbers	Ecclesiastes	Ezekiel
Deuteronomy	Song of Solomon	Daniel
Joshua	**5**	Hosea
Judges	Romans	Joel
Ruth	1 Corinthians	Amos
1 Samuel	2 Corinthians	Obadiah
2 Samuel	Galatians	Jonah
1 Kings	Ephesians	Micah
2 Kings	Philippians	Nahum
1 Chronicles	Colossians	Habakkuk
2 Chronicles	1 Thessalonians	Zephaniah
Ezra	2 Thessalonians	Haggai
Nehemiah	1 Timothy	Zechariah
Esther	2 Timothy	Malachi
17	Titus	**17**
Matthew	Philemon	Revelation
Mark	Hebrews	**1**
Luke	James	
John	1 Peter	
Acts	2 Peter	
5	1 John	
	2 John	
	3 John	
	Jude	
	21	

Esther (beginning with the letter *E*) as the *E*nd of the Old Testament history section. Use the first two letters of the first Bible book, *GE*nesis, to remember that Old Testament history starts with *Genesis* and ends with *Esther*.

The history books are in chronological order and basically relate one continuous story. But the experience and prophecy books are topically grouped, and add various kinds of information to the previously completed historical account. The 22 books between Esther and Matthew provide further details on various periods described between Genesis and Esther.

When you get to the New Testament, the first two letters of the first book, *MA*tthew, will remind you that the New Testament historical story begins with *Matthew* and ends with *Acts*, the fifth book.

All 66 Bible books are laid out topically in the order they appear in our English Bibles on page 10. Note that in both Testaments there are 22 supplements to the story line. (The total number of experience and prophecy books for either Testament is 22.)

The following chart shows at a glance that in the Old Testament, God has emphasized the past and the future (history and prophecy), but in the New Testament the stress is overwhelmingly on our experience with Him and His Word. So in the Old Testament, the "story line" flows through the first 17 books, with the remaining 22 supplementing the narrative.

BOOKS AND TOPICS IN EACH TESTAMENT

O.T. BOOKS	TOPICS	N.T. BOOKS
17	*H* istory	5
5	*E* xperience	21
17	*P* rophecy	1

The Scripture Story

Here's a one-paragraph description of Old Testament history:

After God created everything, He judged the blatant sin of mankind through a worldwide Flood and then scattered men from Babel's tower. Abraham, Isaac, Jacob (Israel), and Joseph were the founding fathers of the Hebrew people. After developing into a great nation and being enslaved in Egypt, the Israelites were delivered under Moses. They were taught, tested, disciplined, and retaught in the wilderness until Joshua led them into their Promised Land. They were ruled by a succession of fourteen judges followed by kings Saul, David, and Solomon. After King Solomon, the Hebrew kingdom was divided into Northern and Southern Kingdoms. After the rules of nineteen wicked kings, Israel was taken from the north and scattered by Assyria. After the rules of twenty southern kings, Judah was taken into captivity in Babylon. While Ezra and Nehemiah were leading the Jews back home to Judah, Esther was a savior-queen in Persia. Four hundred "silent years" passed between that time and the beginning of the New Testament.

Here's a one-paragraph New Testament history:

After a 400-year "silent" period, the biblical account picks up again with the births of John the Baptist and Jesus Christ. After about 30 years, John called the Jewish nation to a baptism of repentance. Jesus Christ, God's flesh-and-blood Son, showed the world what God is like and taught the perfect ways of God for about three years. After preparing twelve disciples to continue His work in the world, Jesus willingly died on a cross for the sins of all mankind, arose from the dead, and returned to heaven. Given power by the Holy Spirit, the disciples spread the Good News about Jesus' salvation, mainly among the Jews. The Apostle Paul carried the Gospel to the Gentiles through extensive missionary journeys and wrote at least thirteen of the New Testament letters. The Apostle John recorded the Revelation, a forward look to God's program for this world till the end of time. The Bible ends as it began—with God completely in charge of His Creation, with no evil opposition.

Draw It Out

The preceding two paragraphs of the Bible story can be summarized on one easy-to-draw map. (If you can draw a crooked line, you can do it!) Examine a modern map to see where in today's world Bible events took place.

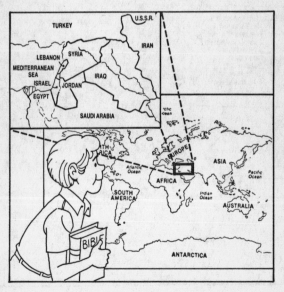

A silly statement helps us remember the names of the rivers and seas which bound the Bible lands: "E.T. purrs in the red tile med." As you follow a clockwise direction from the upper right of the Bible world inset, note the Euphrates and Tigris Rivers, Persian (*Purrs-in*) Gulf, *Red* Sea, Nile (*tile* rhymes), and the Mediterranean Sea. The order of the "E.T." rivers is easy because the *top* one starts with *T*. Just to the east of the Mediterranean Sea is the Sea of Galilee, out of which flows the Jordan River down to the Dead Sea.

An even sillier story helps us draw a map on which we can later summarize the Bible story.

Imagine you are looking at the bow of a fishing boat (line 1). The fishing lines hanging from the boat got all tangled up (lines down to 2). A guy fell out of the boat

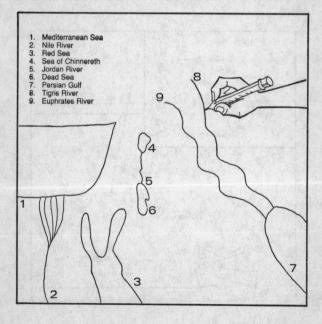

1. Mediterranean Sea
2. Nile River
3. Red Sea
4. Sea of Chinnereth
5. Jordan River
6. Dead Sea
7. Persian Gulf
8. Tigris River
9. Euphrates River

and is standing on the bottom of the shallow lake. All we see of him are his two skinny fingers under the bow of the boat (lines to 3). Being well prepared, he sent a balloon toward the surface, with its string trailing (lines 4 and 5). To keep the balloon from rising too fast, he hung his mitten on the string (line 6). Farther out ahead in the lake is the head of a waterbug (line 7). The bug wants to avoid all the action on his left, so he puts out his two feelers to get safely past (lines 8 and 9).

Trace your finger or pencil over the map lines several times as you reread the above "fish story." Then turn away from the book and practice drawing the whole map. (You don't need to put in the numbers.) Name the water bodies from memory. Here is how one teen (who *is* an artist) drew this freehand map.

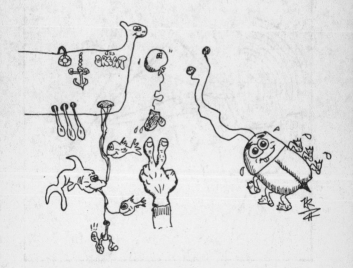

Mapping Out the Scripture Story

Now let's summarize the Bible story simply on our free-hand map. Follow the capital letters and solid lines on the map as you read on.

After God created everything, He placed Adam and Eve in the beautiful Garden of Eden (A—Genesis 2:14 refers to the "E.T." rivers that flowed through the garden). Many other early Bible events happened in this part of the world (Noah's ark and the Tower of Babel, for instance). God called Abraham and Sarah from Ur (B) to Canaan (C—the Promised Land). God made this couple the first Hebrews. (Later most of the Bible would be written by Hebrews; and Jesus was a Jew, a later name for the Hebrews.) The rest of Genesis records the lives of Abraham, Isaac, Jacob and Joseph,

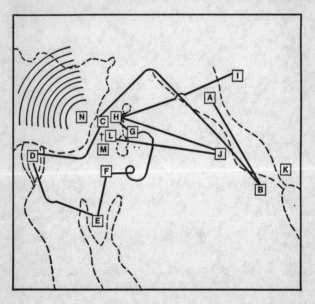

who lived most of their lives in Canaan until Joseph was sold into Egypt (D).

After the Hebrews became a great nation in Egypt and were made slaves, God used ten plagues and Moses to deliver them. Their journey took them through the Red Sea to Mount Sinai (E). They were taught and tested in the wilderness (F). Once the Hebrew nation crossed the Jordan River (G), they settled for centuries (about eight of them) in Canaan (H). General Joshua conquered the land starting with the walls of Jericho. After many judges—including such heroes as Gideon, Samson, and Samuel—came kings Saul, David, and Solomon.

After Solomon, the Hebrew kingdom split in two, with the northern section, Israel, later conquered by Assyria (I—their capital city of Nineveh was on the Tigris River). The southern Jewish kingdom, Judah, was later conquered by Babylon and exiled (J—on the Euphrates River). Seventy years later Persia (K) conquered Babylon, and allowed the Jews to return to Judah (L).

About four centuries later Jesus came as the God-Man to die on a cross for our sins (M—cross symbol), rose from the dead, and returned to heaven. Jesus' disciples (including the Apostle Paul, appointed later) spread the Gospel to the northwest of Israel (N—semicircles radiating from Jerusalem). The Gospel is still being spread across the world by Jesus' modern disciples.

Practice drawing the above Bible summary lines on your freehand map to capture the flow of Bible history.

Test Your Understanding

How well do you think you understand the major message of the Bible? What's the purpose of the Bible's

66 books, 1,189 chapters, 31,173 verses, 774,776 words, and 3,567,180 letters? One good answer: to reveal God and His way of salvation.

If you had to summarize the Scripture's teaching about salvation, what would you say? Any answer that gives people credit (do good, keep the Ten Commandments, obey the Golden Rule) misses the Bible boat. The major message of the Bible is that God offers a *free gift* of salvation to all people, who are helpless to earn it on their own.

The Old Testament got the world ready to respond to Jesus' first coming. The rest of the Bible is about what He can do for us before He comes again. While the focus of this book is the Old Testament, it's important to pause and understand the central New Testament message. It's a message the entire Old Testament leads up to: "These are written that you may believe that Jesus is the Christ, the Son of God, and that by believing you may have life in His name. . . . For God so loved the world that He gave His One and only Son, that whoever believes in Him shall not perish but have eternal life" (John 20:31; 3:16).

But what does it mean to "believe" in Jesus? Many teens familiar with Bible stories are in danger of missing eternal life and heaven by about twelve inches: the distance between the head and the heart. To know the facts about Jesus dying on a cross for our sins is not enough. We must trust Him to forgive our sins as our Saviour.

I enjoy flying. Though I could stand in the airport all day saying how much I believe in a certain airline's planes and pilots, my real belief begins when I get on board and trust my physical destiny to them. Recently I trusted an airline to do something for me I couldn't do for myself: transport me over a thousand miles in less than two hours. And they did it.

Bible belief is trusting Jesus to do some things for us we could never do for ourselves: forgive our sins and give us everlasting life.

Have you ever shifted your hopes of heaven from self to the Saviour? When I was in the seventh grade, I first heard the Good News about Jesus' love for me. I discovered His love was so great that if I were the only sinner who ever needed a Saviour, He still would have died—just for me! But His forgiveness would not be forced on me—I had to choose to receive it as a gift. Though I didn't understand it all, I acted on what little I did know. I confessed I was a sinner and began to trust Jesus to be my Saviour. That was just the beginning of a whole new life—for time and eternity!

Who or what are *you* trusting in?

Thank God for revealing Himself in His special Book, the Bible. Thank Jesus Christ for dying for your sins and trust Him to be *your* Saviour. I can guarantee you from His Word—you'll be glad forever that you did.

2
A SATELLITE VIEW

If the Bible could be likened to a globe of the world with just two great continents, the Old Testament would be bigger, darker, and less explored than the New Testament continent. It's easy to get lost when you're deep in the Old Testament without an overall map. You may find yourself spending an hour studying what amounts to only three trees. Finally you are rescued from the deep forest, only to return to some different but equally confusing spot a week later. This haphazard approach may be great for botanists, but it's frustrating to Bible students!

In this chapter we will look at some satellite shots of three quarters of the Bible. (The Old Testament is over three times the size of the New Testament.) This overview will help provide you with a mental map, so you won't get lost in future visits to the Old Testament.

Designer Books

The first 17 Old Testament books mainly focus on a *past* history that is *national*—dealing with the Hebrew nation. The next 5 books focus more on *present* experiences of *individuals*. The last 17 books focus more on *future* prophecy and bring us back to a *national* scope, since most of the prophets' messages pertain to the Hebrews. These time-terms are relative, of course, since all of the Old Testament is inspired by God for *our* profit today.

The first five books of the Bible are often thought of as a separate segment and are referred to as the "Law" of Moses; or "Torah," a Hebrew word meaning "law"; or "Pentateuch," a Greek word meaning "five scrolls"; or the "Books of Moses," since we believe he was the human author of Genesis through Deuteronomy. Sometimes they are cleverly called "the first five books." When this distinction is drawn, the next 12 books—Joshua through Esther—are considered the history. But there is lots of history in the law, and lots of law in the history; it's just a matter of focus.

The first 5 prophecy books are also often grouped together and called the "major prophets" with the 12 remaining ones called "minor prophets." Is this because the first 5 are more important or more inspired? Not at all—it's simply because the "majors" are much longer. The Book of Jeremiah alone is longer than all 12 minor prophets combined. Isaiah and Ezekiel individually

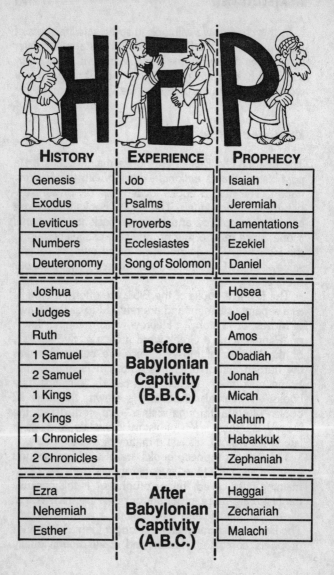

HISTORY	**EXPERIENCE**	**PROPHECY**
Genesis	Job	Isaiah
Exodus	Psalms	Jeremiah
Leviticus	Proverbs	Lamentations
Numbers	Ecclesiastes	Ezekiel
Deuteronomy	Song of Solomon	Daniel
Joshua		Hosea
Judges		Joel
Ruth		Amos
1 Samuel	**Before Babylonian Captivity (B.B.C.)**	Obadiah
2 Samuel		Jonah
1 Kings		Micah
2 Kings		Nahum
1 Chronicles		Habakkuk
2 Chronicles		Zephaniah
Ezra	**After Babylonian Captivity (A.B.C.)**	Haggai
Nehemiah		Zechariah
Esther		Malachi

come within a few pages of equaling the "minors" together.

Note on page 22 the Old Testament's arrangement of the 3 groups of 5 (across the top of the chart) and 2 groups of 12 under them.

After the Pentateuch, the next 9 history books take place before the Babylonian Captivity as do the first 9 of the minor prophets. These 18 books could be called "BBC" (*Before Babylonian Captivity*). The last 3 history books as well as the last 3 prophecy books are "ABC" (*After Babylonian Captivity*).

Notice the perfect balance in the way our English Old Testament is arranged! Even though our order of the books is different from what the Hebrews originally had, we can see the orderly hand of the Heavenly Designer overruling. Our arrangement comes from the Greek version of the Old Testament, the Septuagint, made about 250 years before Christ.

Keeping the Order

Can you name the 39 Old Testament books in order? If so, you've been a good Sunday School scholar. If not, you can use the easy memory aids in this chapter to master this very basic knowledge.

I was in my last year of seminary and still couldn't recite all 66 books of the Bible from memory. Then I was warned this would make a good question for my ordination examination for ministry recognition. I realized it *would* be rather embarrassing to receive a Master's degree in Theology and not be able to even recite the Bible books. So I crammed hard; then no one bothered to ask me!

On page 24 are the 39 Old Testament books set to music in their topical groupings. Though lacking music-

LET US SING

THE MUSICAL LAW

Genesis, Exodus,
  Then comes Leviticus,
Numbers, Deuteronomy,
  And that is the Law!

Let us sing the Books of Moses,
  Of Moses, of Moses,
Let us sing the Books of Moses,
  Of which there are five.

THE MUSICAL HISTORY BOOKS

(Note: chorus repeats a second time)
Let us sing the books of his-try,
  Of his-try, of his-try,
Let us sing the books of his-try,
  Of which there are 12.

There's Joshua and Judges,
  The story of Ruth,
First and Second Samuel,
  And then come the Kings.
The Chronicles follow,
  Then Ezra the scribe,
Then comes Nehemiah,
  And Esther the queen!

THE MUSICAL POETRY BOOKS

Let us sing the books of poe-try,
  Po-et-ry, po-et-ry,
Let us sing the books of poe-try,
  Of which there are five.

Job, Psalms, and Proverbs,
  And then Ecclesiastes.
Solomon's Song follows
  To close this section.

THE MUSICAL MAJOR PROPHETS

Let us sing the Major Prophets,
  The Prophets, the Prophets,
Let us sing the Major Prophets,
  Of which there are five.

Isaiah, Jeremiah,
  Who wrote Lamentations,
Ezekiel and Daniel,
  Both true to their God.

THE MUSICAL MINOR PROPHETS

(Note: chorus repeats a second time)
Let us sing the Minor Prophets,
  The Prophets, the Prophets,
Let us sing the Minor Prophets,
  Of which there are 12.

Hosea and Joel
  And Amos, the shepherd
Obadiah, Jonah, Micah,
  And Nahum also.
Habakkuk, Zephaniah,
  And there was Haggai
Zechariah and Malachi
  To close out the list.

ally, this song makes a good memory device. The tune is "Did You Ever See a Lassie," but we'll call it "Let Us Sing."

If you only want help on the order of the nine pre-Captivity history books, recall them by singing "J J R 2 S K C" to the tune of "Twinkle, Twinkle, Little Star." These letters refer to Joshua, Judges, Ruth, and the two books each of Samuel, Kings, and Chronicles.

For the twelve minor prophets, simply pull off the first two letters of each: Hosea, Joel, Amos, Obadiah, Jonah, Micah, Nahum, Habakkuk, Zephaniah, Haggai, Zechariah, and Malachi. Listed as follows, these letters can be recited as three lines of poetry. Note the lines have three, four, and five syllables as you proceed down.

> Ho Jo Am
> Ob Jo Mi Na
> Ha Ze Ha Ze Ma

There is also a crutch in every Bible that can help when you have to find Zephaniah fast in a service. It's called the table of contents. What is the only thing that might keep us from using it in a group setting and letting our fingers do the walking? You're right—pride! Without pride getting in the way, we can learn lots more and locate Bible books faster.

A Symbolic Scripture Summary

The number 12 crops up several times in our study. There are 12 letters in the words "Old Testament," as well as 12 Hebrew tribes. The following 12 symbols help summarize the Old Testament's 17 history books. These 12 symbols also form the structure of this book, and each is tied to a specific period of Old Testament time. If you're especially sharp you've noticed that as a

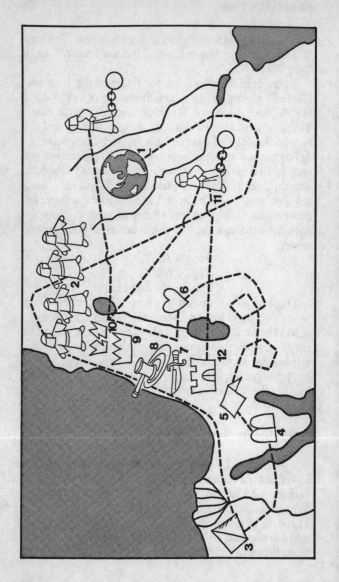

memory-aid, each era begins with the letter "C."

1. **CREATION** (Genesis 1—11). After completing His Creation in six days, God deals with the world as a unit. Adam, Abel, and Noah are key men before the Tower of Babel.

2. **CLAN** (Genesis 12—50). God begins the Hebrew nation with Abraham, who moves to Canaan, and continues it with Isaac, Jacob, and Joseph.

3. **CONFINEMENT** (Exodus 1—19). The Hebrews multiply in Egyptian bondage and are miraculously delivered to Mount Sinai.

4. **COMMANDMENTS** (Exodus 20—Leviticus 27). After the top 10 commandments, God gives 603 more for all areas of successful living.

5. **CAMPING** (Numbers). Unbelief causes the Hebrews to camp in the wilderness for 40 years.

6. **COVENANT** (Deuteronomy). The new generation of Israelites agrees to love God and keep His commandments.

7. **CONQUEST** (Joshua). The Hebrews conquer Canaan and divide it among their 12 tribes.

8. **CYCLES** (Judges—1 Samuel 8). Fourteen deliverers and rulers are raised up during repetitive sin cycles of the Hebrew nation.

9. **CROWNS** (1 Samuel 9—1 Kings 11; 1 Chronicles 1—2 Chronicles 9). Three kings—Saul, David, and Solomon—rule over a united Hebrew kingdom.

10. **CHASM** (1 Kings 12—2 Kings 16; 2 Chronicles 10—28). Rival kings reign over the divided Hebrew kingdoms of Israel and Judah.

11. **CAPTIVITIES** (2 Kings 17—25; 2 Chronicles 29—36). Israel is scattered by Assyria and Judah is later exiled by Babylonia.

12. **CONSTRUCTION** (Ezra—Esther). Judah comes back to Canaan to rebuild Jerusalem and the temple.

The Sequel to the Story

To complete the picture, here is a summary of the rest
of the Scripture story in four additional eras. The 400
years between Testaments and 12 periods for the New
Testament are developed in the companion volume,
New Testament Express.

13. **CLOSED.** During the 400 years between the
Testaments, there are no more direct revelations
through the prophets.

14. **CHRIST** (Matthew 1—Acts 1). Jesus Christ
lives in the world as the God-Man, dies for the sins of
the world, and returns to heaven.

15. **CHURCH** (Acts 2—Revelation 3). The Gospel
is spread through apostles' journeys and letters.

16. **CULMINATION** (Revelation 4—22). A world-

wide Great Tribulation is followed by Christ's return and kingdom.

As you study the Old Testament, you'll find it helpful to have these one-word summaries on the tip of your memory. One easy way to learn these is to recite the 12 Old Testament era names as you point to their corresponding symbols on the map. Practice drawing the symbols on your freehand map. It doesn't matter how crude your symbols may appear—as long as *you* recognize them!

See the story through these 12 periods. After the *CREATION* (1) of the universe, God placed Adam and Eve in a perfect world. Repeated rebellions by mankind caused three great judgments (Eden, Flood, and the Tower of Babel). While the world's nations were developing, God chose Abraham to be the head of a new Hebrew *CLAN* (2). His descendants (Isaac, Jacob, and Joseph) lived in Canaan before moving to Egypt for their *CONFINEMENT* (3) for 400 years. After the plagues on Pharaoh, Moses led the Israelites through the Red Sea to Mount Sinai, where God gave His *COMMANDMENTS* (4) and way to worship. After *CAMPING* (5) for a generation in the wilderness in unbelief, Israel made a *COVENANT* (6) with God near the Jordan River. Joshua led the *CONQUEST* (7) of Canaan and settlement of the Hebrew tribes. *CYCLES* (8) of bondage and deliverance by judges resulted in three men wearing *CROWNS* (9) as kings of the Hebrews. The fourth king, Rehoboam, caused a *CHASM* (10) in the kingdom which continued until both Israel and Judah entered their *CAPTIVITIES* (11). Only Judah returned to Jerusalem for the *CONSTRUCTION* (12) of the temple and city walls. The next communication from God, the New Testament, came only after a 400-year time gap.

The remaining 22 Old Testament books (Job—Mal-

CREATION
2000 + years
Genesis 1—11

CLAN
350 years
Genesis 12—50
(+ Job)

CONFINEMENT
400 years
Exodus 1—19

COMMANDMENTS
2 years
Exodus 20—Leviticus 27

CAMPING
40 years
Numbers

COVENANT
1 month
Deuteronomy

CONQUEST
14 years
Joshua

CYCLES
350 years
Judges—1 Samuel 8

CROWNS
120 years
1 Samuel 9—1 Kings 11
(+ 1 Chronicles 1—
2 Chronicles 9;
Psalms—Song of Solomon)

CHASM
200 years
1 Kings 12—2 Kings 16
(+ 2 Chronicles 10—28;
Isaiah: Hosea—Micah)

CAPTIVITIES
200 years
2 Kings 17—25
(+ 2 Chronicles 29—36;
Jeremiah—Daniel;
Nahum—Zephaniah)

CONSTRUCTION
120 years
Ezra—Esther
(+ Haggai—Malachi)

achi) will be placed in their proper period as we proceed. But if you want to know now where they fit, check the chart on page 30.

A New Way to Read

You can inject some meaningful variety into your Bible-reading diet by taking the books in the order of events. You could read all the Scripture for each of the 12 time periods before moving to the next. Or you could get the big Old Testament picture by reading the first 17 books (Genesis—Esther). Then go back and supplement your reading with the books listed under each.

To get an even better personal overview of the Old Testament, make up your own short, summary title for each biblical chapter you read. I recommend using four words or less, much like a headline for a newspaper article. For example, Genesis 1 could be simply "Creation in Six Days." Chapter 2 might be "Adam and Eve's Garden," with chapter 3 titled "Serpent, Sin, and Penalties." It's not hard to do, and you'll be pleasantly surprised at how much more you'll get out of your reading.

You'll also retain more. Making titles is a cure for mental teflon (you know—not enough is sticking). Titling also helps you understand the big ideas in each chapter's forest instead of getting lost looking at individual verse or paragraph trees. What if there is too much action for a four-word summary? Try titling paragraphs in longer chapters. Then lift ideas from the paragraph titles to make a chapter title.

A further fun step is to turn your chapter title summaries into an acrostic for that Bible book. Here's how it works: Choose a theme for the whole book which has the same number of letters as there are chapters in the book. Then fit each chapter title to the letters in the theme, in order. It's a good mental exercise—rewording chapter titles to fit a new first letter and still have each recall the big idea(s) of the chapter.

To make an acrostic out of a short book such as Ruth, you only need one four-letter word; for example, "Ruth," "Boaz," or "Home." Using the first as an example, Phyllis Hand restated her chapter titles thus:

Return to Judean homeland
Unbelievable kindness of Boaz
Threshing-floor engagement
Happy homelife with Boaz

Look at how a longer book, such as Judges, could be summarized in an acrostic. The Judges example was done by Barry Huddleston, who did the whole Bible this way while in his teens. Appropriately, it's called *The Acrostic Bible*, published by Thomas Nelson. (You can get a copy of *The Acrostic Bible* at a Christian bookstore, or order it for $5, postpaid, from Media Ministries, 516 E. Wakeman, Wheaton, IL 60187.)

JUDGES

3

GETTING IT ALL GOING

CREATION Era (Genesis 1—11)

Genesis is the seed-plot of the garden of Scripture. All major Bible themes have their roots in the Book of Genesis. Just pause and ponder how much information about God and His working we'd miss if the Bible began with Exodus, the second book. Genesis records the beginning of everything except God! A few of the Genesis "firsts" include sun, moon, stars, world, plants, animals, man, woman, marriage, childbirth, and salvation.

The *CREATION* period (Genesis 1—11) covers at least 2,000 years of human history. It can be summarized in four words (three people and one place): Adam, Abel, Noah, and Babel. I remember them as "AANB," picturing a radio tower on the *CREATION* era globe symbol with the call letters "AANB."

The focus of the *CREATION* period is people. People are the principal players in the events of Creation, the Fall from God's fellowship, the worldwide Flood, and the beginning of separate nations at the Tower of Babel. How many people and events can you identify from the *CREATION* era symbols on page 36?

In the Beginning

You've heard the age-old question, "Which came first, the chicken or the egg?" In studying Genesis we learn the original Creation was mature as soon as it was spoken into existence. God created full-grown vegetation with the ability to reproduce itself (Genesis 1:12). So which came first? God's creation pattern suggests the chicken came first with the ability to reproduce through eggs.

A brief summary of Genesis 1 and 2 might go like this:

☐ Day 1—God creates light and basic matter.
☐ Day 2—God makes air and water.
☐ Day 3—God creates land and plants.
☐ Day 4—God sets the sun, moon, and stars.
☐ Day 5—God invents birds and fish.
☐ Day 6—God creates animals and man.

In reading the Creation account it's natural to wonder why God spent six days making the world. He could have saved time; all Creation could have been completed in an instant at His command. But God tells us He planned the process to be a picture of how our week should go: six days of work and one day of worship and rest (Exodus 20:8-11).

God's incredible creative act—making the earth, people, plants, animals, everything—should provide a real boost to our faith. If we recognize that God is big

enough to create the universe in six days, we should have no problem accepting resurrections, healings, or other miracles beyond our understanding.

Besides, how much faith does it take to believe that an eyeball or a kidney could evolve of itself? Think of the faith required to accept an evolutionary explanation for the thousands of complex systems and mechanisms in the human body alone—not to mention their development in both male and female forms! Sorry, but I can't muster enough faith to believe it all just happened apart from a Master Creator.

Adam, God's First Man (Genesis 1-3)

After revealing the first five days of Creation, the Scriptures begin the story of mankind. In the first two chapters of Genesis, God averages less than five verses each for the first five days of the Creation account; yet He gives six times the space to day six, when He made man and woman! After inspecting the quality of each day's work, God said, "Good!" But on day six, after making man, He said nothing. Could that be because God's work wasn't yet complete? Only after making the first woman did God say, "Very good!"

Did you ever stop to wonder why God made us? It's staggering to consider that the eternal and self-sufficient God should make puny mortals to relate to. Yet the world was made for people; even the seventh Sabbath Day was made for man. People were created for fellowship with God.

Adam and Eve are probably most famous for eating the forbidden fruit. Was it an apple? Who knows? But it seems unlikely that anyone would plunge the world into sin for a bite of lemon! Who sinned first? No, not Eve, but the serpent who introduced sin to the first human family. Isaiah 14:12-15 tells more about Satan, the serpent, and his fall from the heights of heaven to the depths of evil.

Genesis also tells us who will win in the cosmic conflict between the forces of good and evil: "I will put enmity between you [the serpent] and the woman, and between your offspring and hers; he will crush your head and you will strike his heel" (Genesis 3:15). Read Revelation for the full account of the outcome, written perhaps 2,000 years before the actual events take place.

By deliberate choice, both Adam and Eve rebelled against God's clear command and fell away from a close communion with their Creator. They had to live with the consequences. Read Genesis 3 and 4 for a catalog of the results of their poor choice, including hard work, pain, sorrow, and death.

Even under the most perfect conditions—such as the Garden of Eden—people tend to turn away from dependence on and delight in the Creator. Left to themselves, people usually choose to be unfaithful to God.

Would you have made a different decision in the Garden than Eve or Adam made? While a piece of fruit, or even knowledge, may not seem so tempting, what if Satan offered you an expensive sports car, the mansion of your dreams, or that person you idolize? Do you have a breaking point, at which you would be willing to sell even your soul?

Just as God sought His first man and woman to have fellowship with them (Genesis 3:9), so He has been seeking people ever since (John 4:23). Are you allowing God, your Creator, to enjoy a personal relationship with you? He is always at hand and ready for fellowship; it is we who sometimes walk away from the Garden.

Abel—Man's First Sacrifice (Genesis 4—5)

Adam and Eve's first two children showed two ways to approach the holy God: His way and man's way. God had evidently made it clear that sinful humans can only approach Him with a blood sacrifice on their behalf. While Abel's animal offering was accepted by God, Cain's substitution of a vegetable offering was rejected.

Everyone who has ever lived since has followed either Cain or Abel. If we trust in our own goodness or works to win God's acceptance, we are following Cain's path. We can't earn our way to heaven through good behavior. There is only one way the sin penalty is paid: by trusting in the sacrifice of Another's blood in place of our own. This is God's plan to restore us to Himself.

Through the death of His holy Son, Jesus Christ,

THE DIFFERENCE BETWEEN RELIGION AND CHRISTIANITY

God has provided the perfect sacrifice once and for all for the sins of the world (Hebrews 9:11-12). How amazing that God's own Son would come Himself and die on a cross to pay for the sins of a rebellious race! Are we important to God? Look at the Creation; look at the Cross.

Who did the first killing in the Bible? *God* killed an animal first to make garments of animal skin for Adam and Eve after their sin. At the same time He apparently was providing a sacrifice for their sin (Genesis 3:21). God was teaching His mortals a basic principle which would be repeated throughout Scripture: without the shedding of blood there is no forgiveness of sin. Abel next killed an animal for a sacrifice. Cain's murder of brother Abel was the third killing in human history.

Noah – God's First Shipbuilder (Genesis 6 – 10)

As the family of man grew, more and more people turned from God. Finally, the human race became so bad that God said, "I will wipe mankind, whom I have created, from the face of the earth" (Genesis 6:7). A worldwide flood would be God's tool to clean the earth of all but a few remaining believers. So God had Noah go to work building a huge boat called an ark.

Noah did what God asked, even though it probably did not seem reasonable to him. How ridiculous his landlocked shipbuilding project must have seemed to his unbelieving neighbors! Who had ever seen or heard of such a thing as a flood?

While the giant ship was the big joke of Noah's neighborhood, it was actually God's means to give the human race a new beginning. At 75 feet wide, 450 feet long, and three stories high, the ark had more floor

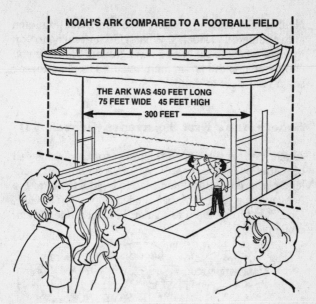

NOAH'S ARK COMPARED TO A FOOTBALL FIELD

THE ARK WAS 450 FEET LONG
75 FEET WIDE   45 FEET HIGH
← 300 FEET →

space than a modern football field.

Even allowing plenty of space for all possible animal species as well as the food and disposal systems needed to stay afloat for a year and 10 days, it's been estimated that the ark sailed at least two thirds empty!

Why did God have Noah make the ark so big? What was Noah doing for over 100 years besides building a boat? He was warning the world of coming judgment. There was room enough on the ark for anyone who responded to Noah's call to enter the only door of physical salvation. But people stayed away. Only Noah and his family believed God; everyone else continued to eat, drink, and be merry (see Matthew 24:37-39). When the rains stopped, the entire world population was down to eight.

We who are alive today owe our very existence to

Noah's believing and obeying God. Consider your own faith compared to Noah's. What is God revealing to you that He wants to do in and through your life? Are you cooperating with Him in faith, even if His plan doesn't seem fully clear to you?

Babel—Man's First Skyscraper (Genesis 11)

Again, people substituted their plan for God's. Instead of scattering over the earth as God commanded, mankind clustered in Babel and tried to build a tower to the heavens as a symbol of their unified opposition to God. God didn't force them to scatter; He just made it more convenient!

Before Babel the whole world spoke one language. Picture the confusion: one morning Joe, working on the 49th floor, calls to Harry on 48 for more bricks. "Acht du lieber!" "Qu'est-ce que c'est?" The whole building project ground to a halt when the workers couldn't communicate. God frustrated their rebellious efforts by twisting their tongues. People who could understand one another got together and moved off to start their own civilization.

Genesis 1—11 is filled with interesting Bible trivia. As you read these chapters, see if you can spot:

☐ The man with the first permanent identification mark (Genesis 4:15),

☐ The world's first polygamist (Genesis 4:19),

☐ The oldest man who ever lived (Genesis 5:27),

☐ The 365-year-old man who disappeared while taking a walk with God (Genesis 5:24),

☐ The founder of Nineveh, where Jonah later preached (Genesis 10:8-11).

In the early days of human history, God repeatedly demonstrated that the clay must submit to the command of the potter. If Moses were to summarize in one sentence his advice for us from the *CREATION* era, it might be, "Creatures are subject to their Creator."

4

FOUR GREAT MEN

CLAN Era (Genesis 12—50)

God must like people. After all, He made so many of them! (And judging by some of the creatures He made, God must have a great sense of humor too.)

If you were to try to list from memory all the people mentioned in the Bible, how many do you think you could name? 100? 200? 500? If so, you would be a little short. There are 2,930 *different* people woven into the Word of God (not including the great number of multiple mentions)! And if *your* name appeared in one of those Bible lists, how would you like people to skip over it?

God's focus is people! Sure, *God* created the heavens and the earth. But He trusted *people* to cultivate the Garden of Eden (Genesis 2:15), name the animals (Genesis 2:20), and reproduce to cover the earth (Genesis 9:1). Even today, God works through His people in your community, your church, and your family. We tend to look for new methods to work, but God looks for available men and women through whom *He* can work.

Genesis — "Generations to Joseph"

In spite of all the great one-and-only events in Genesis, *people* are the primary focus. The generations from Adam to Joseph are detailed, with lengthy footage given to Adam, Eve, Abel, Cain, Seth, Noah, Abraham, Isaac, Jacob, and Joseph. Genesis carries us from the creation of Adam to the coffin of Joseph; from freedom in Eden to Egypt and preparation for bondage.

Can you identify these noteworthy people from the pages of Genesis?

☐ Sent by his brothers on an all-expense-paid tour of the pyramids

☐ Narrowly missed being killed by his father

☐ Only person in the Bible called "the friend of God"

☐ Fathered 13 children by two wives and two concubines. (*Unger's Bible Dictionary* defines a *concubine* as "a secondary or inferior wife.")

(Answers are given throughout the rest of this chapter.)

The first two big Bible periods (*CREATION* and *CLAN*) are found in the Book of Genesis. Chapters 1—11 cover the whole world, but 12—50 center in Canaan after Abraham's migration from near the Persian Gulf. The *CREATION* era begins the story of sin in the human race, but the *CLAN* era begins the story of salvation to come through the Hebrew race and Abraham's ultimate descendant, Jesus Christ. From chapter 12 on, Genesis is devoted to the lives of four men: Abraham, Isaac, Jacob, and Joseph (the four founding fathers of the Hebrew clan). All four were later remembered in "God's Hall of Faith" (address: Hebrews 11, New Testament).

Abraham—Friend of God (Genesis 12—25)

After mankind repeatedly demonstrated a tendency toward sin (Genesis 3—11), God called a man named Abram (later called Abraham) from a highly developed pagan civilization to become the head of the new Hebrew nation (Genesis 12:1-3). Don't ever *err* about his hometown (Ur—Genesis 11:31)!

In response to God's call, Abraham and his family migrated up the fertile crescent to Haran in Mesopotamia, later into Canaan (the Promised Land), and finally into Egypt. So Genesis goes from Eden to Egypt.

Did God choose Abraham and his Hebrew descendants because they were better than other people? Paul answers with a big no (Romans 4). Abraham had to receive his righteousness and acceptance as a gift from God, just like everyone else (Genesis 15:6).

But of the 2,930 people mentioned in the Bible, Abraham is the only one referred to as "friend of God" (2 Chronicles 20:7; Isaiah 41:8; James 2:23). He is revered by both Jews and Arabs as the father of their race (through his sons, Isaac and Ishmael, respectively). See Abraham's family tree on page 48.

God promised Abraham a great name, a large family, and a blessing on the whole earth through him (Genesis 12:1-3). God renewed these great promises to

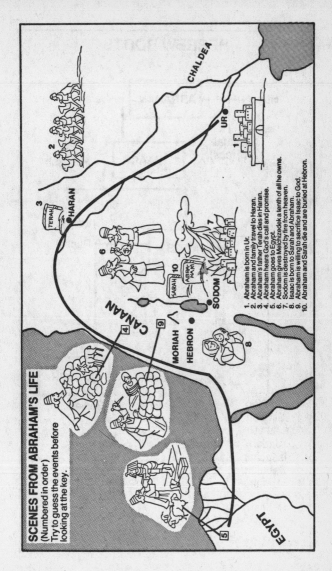

SCENES FROM ABRAHAM'S LIFE

(Numbered in order.)
Try to guess the events before
looking at the key.

CHALDEA

UR

HARAN
TERAH

CANAAN

MORIAH

HEBRON

SODOM

SARAH ABRA-HAM

EGYPT

1. Abraham is born in Ur.
2. Abraham and family travel to Haran.
3. Abraham's father Terah dies in Haran.
4. Abraham hears God's call and promise.
5. Abraham goes to Egypt.
6. Abraham gives Melchizedek a tenth of all he owns.
7. Sodom is destroyed by fire from heaven.
8. Isaac is born to Sarah and Abraham.
9. Abraham is willing to sacrifice Isaac to God.
10. Abraham and Sarah die and are buried at Hebron.

47

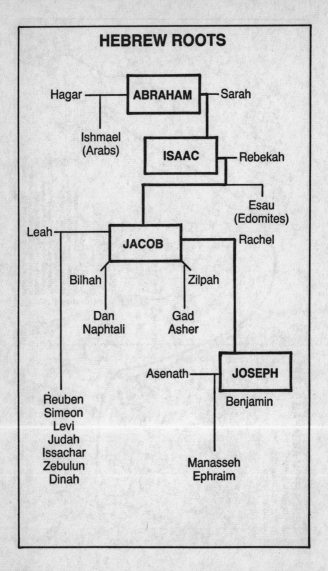

HEBREW ROOTS

Hagar — **ABRAHAM** — Sarah

Ishmael
(Arabs)

ISAAC — Rebekah

Esau
(Edomites)

Leah — **JACOB** — Rachel

Bilhah — Zilpah

Dan
Naphtali

Gad
Asher

Asenath — **JOSEPH**

Benjamin

Reuben
Simeon
Levi
Judah
Issachar
Zebulun
Dinah

Manasseh
Ephraim

Abraham's son Isaac (Genesis 17:19), his grandson Jacob (Genesis 35:10-12), and his great grandson Joseph (Genesis 49:22-26).

Abraham's faith was evident through his obedience to God. He left Ur without knowing his destination, because he knew God was leading the way. After settling 900 miles away in Canaan, he believed God would give him a son, even though his wife, Sarah, was long past childbearing years.

Abraham's faith was put to the ultimate test when he climbed Mount Moriah and was willing to sacrifice his son, Isaac, at God's command. Abraham knew that God would not break His promise to give Abraham a large family, even if He had to raise Isaac from the dead (Hebrews 11:17-19). And God rewarded Abraham's faith by providing a substitute sacrifice (Genesis 22:10-13).

Does this mean we have to be perfect to follow Abraham's great example of a faith that works? Not at all. Abraham's faith was more like a roller-coaster ride than a rocket headed toward the moon. Twice he said his wife was his sister to protect himself (Genesis 12:11-20 and 20:1-18). (Sarah *was* his half sister, but Abraham's intentional deception cannot be commended.)

Another time Abraham slept with Sarah's servant, Hagar, and became the father of Ishmael. Isaac's descendants became the Jews and Ishmael's descendants became the Arabs, so the effects of Abraham's sin are still felt today. But overall, Abraham's faith is an example we should all try to imitate.

Faith without works (actions) is dead and useless (James 2:26). Abraham acted on his faith. He left his homeland. He trusted God for a child. He was willing to sacrifice that child if that had been what God wanted. Abraham's faith worked. Does yours?

Isaac—A Submissive Son (Genesis 26)

The Bible tells us less about Isaac than his famous father (Abraham), his son Jacob, or his grandson Joseph. Genesis contains only sporadic snapshots of Isaac. Genesis 26 is devoted to him, but most of what we know about Isaac is in relation to his other family members. Yet Isaac is a crucial link to continue Abraham's clan toward Christ. (See Abraham's family tree on page 48.)

Isaac was miraculously born to a 90-year-old mother and a 100-year-old father (Genesis 17:17). When he was about 17, he was willing to be bound by his father, placed on an altar, and sacrificed to God. (Read the news release in Genesis 22.) But don't you imagine he was thankful that Abraham's century-old ears could hear the angel in time to prevent the sacrifice? Isaac later followed his dad's example of faith by believing God's promises and taking a Hebrew wife (Rebekah—Genesis 24).

When I was a teenager, I was once troubled over a girl who wasn't as interested in me as I thought she should be. In fact, she seemed more interested in another guy. So I decided to pray for him. (I prayed that God would use an auto accident, heart attack, or any other means of His sovereign choice to remove him from the scene!) But the more I tried to ask God to intervene, the more miserable I became.

Then I heard a sermon about Abraham offering Isaac to God. I decided to build my own altar (in my mind, in prayer to God) and picture my girlfriend there. I wanted God to know I trusted Him to do what was best with her. I knew if God took her away, He could provide someone better for me. Great peace and joy followed. I was free to love both my girlfriend *and* the other guy and wish God's best on them.

I had to rebuild my altar several times in the months that followed. I kept tearing it down during lapses of doubt and unbelief. But God honored my commitment. A few years later I married the girl on the altar!

Life doesn't always work out so painlessly. Sometimes God "consumes" what is sacrificed to Him. (Ask me sometime about my classic '55 Ford or my Leica camera.) But I have discovered that every time God takes something away from me, He always gives me something better (though sometimes the replacement comes much later).

Isaac had no doubts about God's faithfulness. In his supernatural birth, obedience unto death (by submission to his father), and victory over death, Isaac bears a likeness to Christ.

Jacob—Saint in the Rough (Genesis 27—36)

How many scenes from Jacob's life can you identify in the composite picture on page 52?

Jacob is remembered as a schemer. He is probably most famous for talking his brother, Esau, into trading his firstborn inheritance status for a bowl of stew. But he also schemed against his father (Genesis 27) and his father-in-law, Laban (Genesis 30:25—31). If you are beginning to think scheming might be a successful way to get ahead, take a look at Jacob's 20 wasted years in Haran, working for a bigger schemer, Laban. Jacob's father-in-law switched daughters on Jacob's wedding day so Jacob would have to work twice as long to get the one he wanted (Genesis 29). And some of Jacob's sons picked up on dad's tricks and became schemers themselves (Genesis 34).

Jacob had 13 children by two wives (Leah and Rachel) and his wives' handmaids (Bilhah and Zilpah).

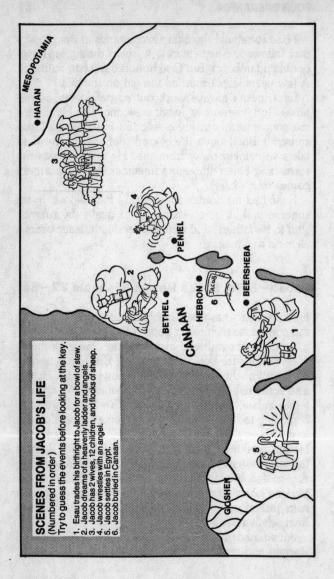

SCENES FROM JACOB'S LIFE
(Numbered in order)
Try to guess the events before looking at the key.

1. Esau trades his birthright to Jacob for a bowl of stew.
2. Jacob dreams of a heavenly ladder and angels.
3. Jacob has 2 wives, 12 children, and flocks of sheep.
4. Jacob wrestles with an angel.
5. Jacob settles in Egypt.
6. Jacob buried in Canaan.

MESOPOTAMIA

HARAN

PENIEL

BETHEL

CANAAN

HEBRON

JACOB

BEERSHEBA

GOSHEN

His 12 sons originated the 12 tribes of Israel. ("Israel" was the name God gave to Jacob—Genesis 35:10.) He also had one daughter, Dinah. Jacob's family tree is on page 48.

I wonder how Jacob remembered the names of all his sons. Here's how I do it with two sentences: "*A*lways *B*e *D*oing *G*ood, *I*srael-*J*acob. *J*acob's *L*ine *N*ow *R*esponds, *S*howing *Z*eal." (The first letters of these two sentences divide the names equally and put them in alphabetical order.) Below are the "children of Israel," or "Israelites."

Asher	Judah
Benjamin	Levi
Dan	Naphtali
Gad	Reuben
Issachar	Simeon
Joseph	Zebulun

Jacob's son Judah began the tribe that Jesus eventually came from, but Joseph gets the most space in Genesis.

Joseph—Patience Pays (Genesis 37—50)

Joseph can be remembered by what he wore (coat of many colors given as a sign of his father's favoritism), what he dreamed (his family members as heavenly bodies bowing down to him), where he went (to Egypt, sold as a slave by his jealous brothers), and what he became (vice-president of Egypt). Identify the scenes in Joseph's life on page 55.

Does it pay to be faithful to God in spite of injustices done to us? After all, the way Joe's brothers treated him was the "pits" (Genesis 37:24). And innocent Joseph spent years in jail because of a frame-up by a wicked woman (Genesis 39:7-20). Joseph's remarkable response to his life of misfortune is recorded in Genesis 50:20: "You intended to harm me, but God intended it for good to accomplish . . . the saving of many lives." Joseph is an excellent example of the truthfulness of Romans 8:28: "We know that in all things God works for the good of those who love Him."

Since Joseph trusted God to work things out for his good, he could be patient in prison while God was arranging the preservation of the Hebrew race.

Joseph is another great Old Testament picture of Jesus. One Bible student found over 100 ways in which Joseph is like Jesus (he has no recorded sin, he suffered for no wrong of his own, he was a savior of the Hebrews, etc.). You can find many more in the last 14 chapters of Genesis.

Job—Patience Personified

The Book of Job may have been written later, but Job probably lived during this early period recorded in Genesis (the *CLAN* era). Job fits the pattern where average life expectancy was well over 100 and fathers functioned as priests for their families (evidently before Moses and the tabernacle). Since Job had ten children when his troubles came (Job 1:2), and lived another 140 years after his restoration (Job 42:16), he must have been at least 175 when he died.

Job lived in the land of Uz, which Jeremiah associates with Edom, Esau's later homeland south of the Dead Sea (Lamentations 4:21). He was the greatest Old Testament example of patience that James could cite (James 5:11).

Like Joseph, Job suffered greatly due to no fault of

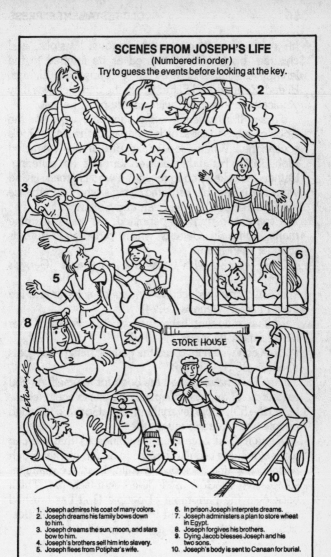

SCENES FROM JOSEPH'S LIFE
(Numbered in order)
Try to guess the events before looking at the key.

1. Joseph admires his coat of many colors.
2. Joseph dreams his family bows down to him.
3. Joseph dreams the sun, moon, and stars bow to him.
4. Joseph's brothers sell him into slavery.
5. Joseph flees from Potiphar's wife.
6. In prison Joseph interprets dreams.
7. Joseph administers a plan to store wheat in Egypt.
8. Joseph forgives his brothers.
9. Dying Jacob blesses Joseph and his two sons.
10. Joseph's body is sent to Canaan for burial.

STORE HOUSE

his own. After losing his possessions, livestock, and children, his troubles increased as he listened to the lengthy dialogues of his visiting counselors: Eliphaz, Bildad, Zophar, and Elihu. But in the end, Job was fully vindicated and blessed with double of all he lost.

To say that suffering is the summary word for the Book of Job is to miss the bigger part of the story: God's sovereignty! When God spoke out of the whirlwind (Job 38:1), He didn't deliver sermons on suffering. Rather, He asked Job to recognize who He really is and what He is capable of doing. That's why I summarize the Book of Job as "Jehovah and Suffering."

If space and purpose permitted, we could examine many stories in Genesis which prove that truth is stranger than fiction:

☐ A woman who became a salt statue (Genesis 19:26)

☐ Two cities reduced to cinders by sulphur and fire from heaven (Genesis 19:24)

☐ The bride who became a reject the morning after her marriage (Genesis 29:20-30)

☐ A con which involved the genetic patterns of goats (Genesis 30:31-43)

You'll just have to read the book for yourself! As you read these exciting 39 chapters of Genesis again (chapters 12—50), note everything that God did through people and what He taught them.

Though God occasionally reminds us that He *can* work alone, He usually chooses to do His work through people. Looking back over my life, I can see many instances where God used others to reach me. Think back over the panorama of people God has brushed across the canvas of your life, and thank Him. (If possible, you might want to thank *them* too!)

5

THE GREAT ESCAPE

CONFINEMENT Era (Exodus 1—19)

Can you think of a Bible personality who:

☐ Rode alone in a boat when only three months old

☐ Grew up around royalty but gave it up for a desert lifestyle

☐ Once saw a bush that burned without being consumed

☐ Used his brother to do his speaking

☐ Represented God to deliver ten plagues and ten commandments

☐ Escaped several death sentences

☐ Is remembered as the meekest man on earth

If Moses came to mind, you're right. He is the major character for the next four Old Testament eras: *CON-*

FINEMENT, COMMANDMENTS, CAMPING, and *COVENANT.*

A suitable three-word theme for the Book of Exodus would be "Exit from Egypt." Below is a synopsis of the *CONFINEMENT* era. (See how many scenes you can identify in the composite map of Exodus 1—19 on page 59.

The 70 Hebrews who entered Egypt in Genesis multiplied to a great multitude during their 400 years in Egypt. (If 70 men doubled every 25 years over a 400-year span, there would be more than 4½ million people.) The Hebrew population explosion worried Pharaoh, who appointed taskmasters over the Israelites. The people cried out to God (Exodus 2:23), and He heard them. That's where Moses comes in.

Humor in Heaven

Does God have a sense of humor? Obviously so, judging by the way He handled Pharaoh (the Egyptian king) when Pharaoh began to enslave the Hebrews and have their male babies killed.

When it was no longer safe to hide Moses at home, his mother placed him in a waterproof basket and floated him down the Nile. Pharaoh's daughter "just happened" to be walking past, Moses "just happened" to cry, and Moses' sister "just happened" to be around to suggest a Hebrew woman (Moses' mother) who could nurse the baby. So Pharaoh's daughter adopted Moses. The same monarch who persecuted the Hebrews paid the expenses (for 40 years) to raise and train the man who was to rescue the Hebrews from their persecution. Any time a human sovereign attempts to frustrate the plans of the heavenly Sovereign, God will always have the last laugh.

THE CONFINEMENT ERA
(Scenes numbered in order)
Try to guess the events before looking at the key.

MEDITERRANEAN SEA

GOSHEN

RED SEA

MIDIAN

MT. SINAI

1. Hebrews make bricks in bondage.
2. Baby Moses hidden in a basket on the Nile River.
3. Moses tends sheep in Midian.
4. Passover: a Hebrew applies blood to doorframe.
5. The Lord leads Israel in a pillar of cloud and fire.
6. The Red Sea is parted.
7. A tree thrown into a pond makes the water drinkable.
8. The Israelites camp at Elim.
9. The Lord provides manna and quail.
10. Moses gets water from a rock.
11. The Lord talks with Moses at Mt. Sinai.

After Moses' first 40 years with Pharaoh, a civil dispute caused him to spend the next 40 years in Midian—beyond the Red Sea (Exodus 2:11-25). At the end of that time, Moses received further orders from God through a burning bush. Teamed up with his brother Aaron to seek the release of the Hebrews, Moses began his main life work at 80 (as did Joshua a generation later).

Think for a moment about the importance God places on proper preparation for our life work. Moses had a ratio of 2:1 (two years of preparation for each year of ministry). Noah had a 5:1 ratio. And Jesus had ten years of preparation for every year of "official" ministry. Perhaps more can be done in less time by someone who has been trained under God's schedule of development.

Help in Making Decisions

God didn't force the stubborn Egyptian king to dismiss his slave labor force. But after Pharaoh's first refusal, God began to send plagues to "encourage" Pharaoh to change his mind. After each plague, Pharaoh could have relented. But instead, his refusals prompted God to send increasingly severe plagues. It finally took the death of his oldest son before Pharaoh gave his permission for the Israelites to leave. (By that time, the Egyptians were more than willing to equip their Hebrew neighbors for travel—Exodus 12:35-36.)

How many of the ten plagues can you name? Can you identify them all from this picture?

Starting with #1, they are:

Nile River turned to blood	Boils on people
	Hail

Frogs   Locusts
Lice   Darkness
Flies   Death of firstborn
Livestock disease   sons

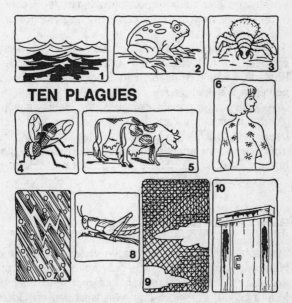

TEN PLAGUES

How did God select His ten plagues? Archeology has confirmed the Nile River, locusts, cattle, etc. were the gods of Egypt. One-by-one, God showed His supremacy over them.

For example, the Egyptians worshiped the sun. *Click!* Intense darkness blankets the land as the sunlight instantly disappears. But just to show it wasn't some "natural" phenomenon, God left the lights on in the Hebrews' homes.

Can you imagine people worshiping frogs? (That's almost as ridiculous as worshiping a car or clothes.)

Since the Egyptians put a higher emphasis on frogs than on the true God, the Lord gave them so many frogs that they were in people's beds, ovens, and even in bread dough as the ladies kneaded it. Every step and squish (and later the huge piles of rotting frogs—Exodus 8:13-14) showed the folly of worshiping creation instead of the Creator.

The last plague, the death of the firstborn in every Egyptian home, was aimed at Egypt's chief god—Pharaoh himself. Pharaoh could not overlook God's power in this final plague.

As with all the previous plagues, the Hebrews were given a means of escape from the last one. But each family had to kill a lamb and apply the blood to their front door so the angel of death would "pass over" that home (Exodus 12). That's how the annual Hebrew Passover ceremony began.

Born Twice—Die Once

The Book of Exodus describes two redemptions of the Hebrew people: their *physical* redemption from Egypt, and their *spiritual* redemption in Egypt (and later at Mount Sinai). Far more emphasis is placed on God's spiritual relationship with His Old Testament people.

Even more important is God's spiritual deliverance of His people from the bondage of sin and death. The Passover and Feast of Unleavened Bread (Exodus 12) were established to keep reminding Israel of their undeserved gift of salvation. And after God brought the people to Mount Sinai, He gave them detailed instructions on how they were to live out their new relationship with Him. (Skim through the 57 chapters between Exodus 19 and Numbers 10 sometime to see *how* detailed.) The Israelites were to be God's "treasured possession. . . . a kingdom of priests and a holy nation" (Exodus 19:5-6). Their physical birth as a nation was supposed to be a prelude to their spiritual birth.

Jesus taught the same principle when He told Nicodemus, a high-ranking religious teacher in Israel, "You must be born again" (John 3:7). Jesus was aware of two different kinds of birth: physical birth (which comes naturally) and spiritual birth (which only comes supernaturally).

Do you have confidence that you are alive spiritually, as well as physically? Just as you have been born once (thanks to your parents), you can have a second birth spiritually (thanks to the provision made through Jesus Christ as your Saviour). No one can ever see the kingdom of God without being born again ("born anew" or "born from above"—John 3:1-16). Just as an

Israelite in Egypt could only be saved from death by sacrificial blood applied to his door, we can only be saved by Christ's blood applied to our sinful account.

Because of Christ's work on the cross, when we *exit* from earth, we can immediately *enter* heaven!

The Great Divide

It's hard to tell for sure how many Israelites left Egypt. Earlier in this chapter we estimated 4½ million based on normal population growth of the original 70 people (Genesis 46:27). But let's use a more conservative estimate of 3½ million. We know there were 600,000 men. Most of these men would be married, so let's double the figure to 1,200,000. An average of four children per couple (4 × 600,000 = 2,400,000) brings us to the 3½ million total (1.2 million + 2.4 million = 3.6 million). Some Bible scholars think that senior citizens were not included in the numbering, and that the number of people who left Egypt could total as many as 6 or 7 million.

The route of the Israelites' exodus went from Egypt through the Red Sea to Mount Sinai (in the Sinai peninsula between the two "fingers" of the Red Sea). How wide was the Red Sea parted? If 3½ million people marched two abreast, it would take them about 35 days and nights to cross the Red Sea. But we know the entire group (with animals and baggage) crossed in a single night (Exodus 14:21).

Because they were laden with the wealth of Egypt and were more of a mob than an organized parade, I believe they may have crossed the Red Sea as many as 5,000 abreast. Even so, the Sea had to be parted at least five miles wide for them all to get across in one night! Of course, these figures are mostly estimated. But it is no wonder the Bible so often refers back to God's mighty miracle of taking His people through the Red Sea. This miracle also gave the heathen Canaanite nations a healthy fear of the Israelites' Almighty God.

To recall two key people, one major event, and the final destination of the *CONFINEMENT* era, remember that the Israelites would need "MAPS" for their journey out of Egypt. These four letters stand for *M*oses, *A*aron, *P*assover (which in turn reminds us of the ten *P*lagues), and *S*inai (which in turn reminds us they had to cross the *S*ea).

Mundane Miracles

These days some people base all their spiritual commitment on physical miracles, even though miracles are rare and only last for a short while. But as the Israelites left Egypt, they were surrounded by miracles. God led them by means of a pillar of cloud by day and a pillar of fire by night (Exodus 14:21-22). He parted the Red Sea (Exodus 14:21-22). He provided bread (manna) in the morning and meat (quails) in the evening (Exodus 16:13, 35). He provided water in unusual ways and from unlikely places (Exodus 15:22-27; 17:6).

What was the response of the recipients? You would expect them to be overwhelmed by protection and provision, right? But they responded with more grumbling than gratefulness; pity parties instead of praise gatherings. The miraculous soon became mundane. It got so bad that the people decided they would rather go back to the slavery of Egypt than the freedom of God's Promised Land (Exodus 14:11-12; 16:2-3; 17:3). (Anybody who lusts for leeks, garlic, and onions *must* be out of fellowship! [See Numbers 11:5-6.])

But before we condemn the Hebrew people too

quickly, perhaps we need to examine our own lives. I used to look down on the Israelites. But the older I get, the more I see my own attitudes reflected in the Israelites' behavior. God can do a mighty miracle for me one day, and I'm grumbling the next!

The wilderness was God's training ground to develop the faith of His Old Testament people. All Israel had to do was believe and obey—two things they were capable of doing. God would handle everything they were incapable of doing themselves.

What's the point for us? God's physical provisions are designed as tangible object lessons to help us comprehend His spiritual provisions. His ability to meet our physical needs should cause us to understand that He is able to meet our spiritual needs as well.

God provided for the physical needs of the Israelites. All they needed to do was believe and obey. Instead, they wanted to return to their old ways, even though they would still be slaves!

We have the same choice: to believe or not, to obey or not. God wants to deliver us from the bondage of sin and give us a freedom that only He can provide. Will you believe and obey, or return to slavery? The choice is yours.

6

SCHOOLED FOR SUCCESS

COMMANDMENTS Era
(Exodus 20—Leviticus 27)

Question: Who was the only person who broke all Ten Commandments in one act? *Answer:* Moses. Remember when he became angry over the golden calf and broke up the stone tablets of Law? (Exodus 32:19)

Here's another trick question. How many commandments were given at Mount Sinai?

    (A) 10
    (B) 20
    (C) 613
    (D) All of the above

The correct answer is (D). We all know that (A) is true because God gave Moses Ten Commandments written on rocks (Exodus 31:18). Another acceptable answer for the number of commandments at Sinai is (B) 20. After Moses smashed the first set, God had to repeat them to Moses later. God did the stone carving the first time (Exodus 32:16), but Moses had to do it the second time! (Exodus 34:27) But after listing the "big" Ten Commandments, God continued without pausing to list a lot more. Exodus and Leviticus contain a total of 613 commandments that were issued at Sinai! So (C) is also correct.

How's Your Command of the Commandments?

Could you name the Ten Commandments in the order God gave them? As you try, see if you can make sense of these symbols as a memory device:

Here's the key to the chart:

1. No other gods
2. No *graven* images
3. No vain (vane?) use of God's name
4. Keep the Sab*bath* Day
5. Honor your parents

6. No killing
7. No adultery (a dull tree?)
8. No stealing
9. No bearing false witness
10. No coveting

Think for a minute about these ten key guidelines for living. They are a significant part of the instruction manual for every human ever produced. Which two commands are stated positively? Which one has a promise attached in the original version in Exodus 20? Which ones govern our relationships to God? Our relationships to other people?

It's interesting that nine of the Ten Commandments are restated in the New Testament as commands for us.

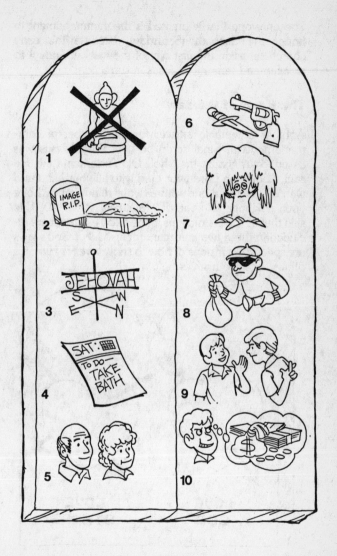

The only one that is omitted is the commandment to
honor the Sabbath (Saturday), because the early
church set aside the first day of the week (Sunday) to
worship and remember Jesus' resurrection.

The Heart of the Law

Another acceptable answer for the number of commandments at Sinai could be two! When Jesus was
asked to summarize the whole Old Testament Law, He
said, "Love the Lord your God with all your heart and
with all your soul and with all your mind," and "Love
your neighbor as yourself" (Matthew 22:37-40). He
said that all the instructions in the Old Testament are included in these two commandments. All of God's laws
are specific extensions of how to show love for Him, for
others, or for ourselves.

LOVE
GOD

LOVE
OTHERS

Read Exodus 20—23 for a concentrated course on how God's guidelines are to be applied to all areas of life: spiritual, social, emotional, and physical. No compartment of life was to be sealed from God's influence; no differentiating between "secular" and "sacred." A Hebrew's relationship to God was to affect *every* facet of his life.

Some interesting sidelights you'll encounter in these chapters include how to:

☐ Build an altar without tools (Exodus 20:24-25)

☐ Pierce ears (Exodus 21:2-6)

☐ Apply the "tooth-for-tooth" principle (Exodus 21:22-27)

☐ Live to a ripe old age (Exodus 23:25-26)

You'll also discover why:

☐ Many young people would have to be killed if these laws were literally legislated today (Exodus 21:15, 17)

☐ Siding with the majority is not always wise (Exodus 23:1-3)

☐ Some collateral on loans can only be held during daylight hours (Exodus 22:26-27)

☐ Hebrew farmers were to get a year's vacation after every seven years of working (Exodus 23:10-11)

3,000 Years Later

You might think the New Testament would contain fewer commandments than the Old Testament, since we're not living under the Law anymore. But the New Testament contains 1,051 commands, most of them in the Books Romans through Jude. Some of these commands are for past or future times or specific people, but most are for us today!

So the next time you read an Old or New Testament

SCENES
AT
SINAI

Letwenko

command that applies to you, mark an exclamation mark (!) beside each one. God's principles work—especially if we work them!

The Ten Commandments (Exodus 20) introduce another 48 chapters of instruction at the Sinai School for Successful Living. Study the picture on page 72 for other elements of the two-year curriculum.

Some unusual events are recorded in Exodus 20—Leviticus 27, such as:

☐ Contributions by goats, sea cows, and rams (Exodus 26:7, 14)

☐ A 12-jeweled vest for making decisions (Exodus 28:15-21, 35)

☐ Payments to avoid a plague (Exodus 30:11-16)

☐ Recipes for incense (Exodus 30:34-38)

☐ A self-made calf (Exodus 32:1-4)

☐ A man wearing a veil (Exodus 34:29-35)

☐ What to eat and what not to eat (Leviticus 11)

☐ Blood used to purify a house (Leviticus 14:48-53)

☐ The first scapegoat (Leviticus 16:20-22)

A Portable Church Building

At Mount Sinai, God also told His people how to build a portable worship center called the tabernacle. Since almost 5 percent of the written content of the Bible describes the tabernacle, it must be an important subject.

At the only entrance was an altar for sacrificing animals, so the tabernacle reminded the people that without the shedding of blood, there is no forgiveness of sin. When viewed from above, all of the "furnishings" of the tabernacle are laid out in the form of a cross. As you study this diagram of the tabernacle, in what other ways do you think it symbolizes Jesus or salvation?

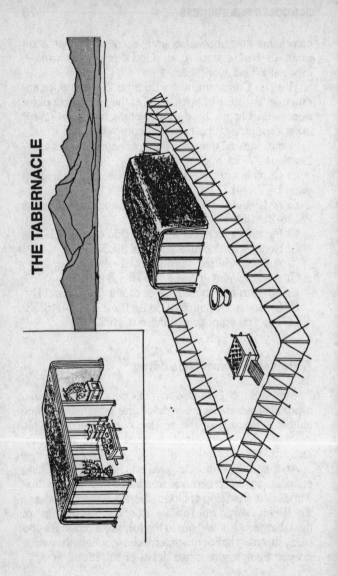

THE TABERNACLE

Leviticus — "Levites and Sacrifices"

God selected the Jewish tribe of Levi to serve as the priests. The word "Leviticus" literally means "pertaining to the Levites." It's no surprise then that the book focuses on Levites and their functions. But as you read through Leviticus, remember that God's people today are also to be priests (1 Peter 2:5, 9; Revelation 1:5-6).

The Book of Leviticus opens with five major kinds of sacrifices for sin and its effects. Seven major annual feasts celebrating God's redemption close the book. Sandwiched between are rules for purity in all areas of life. The spiritual highlight of the year was the Day of Atonement (Leviticus 16). God's goal for the Levites was that His holiness be reflected in His people. This purpose is evident in their sacrifices and feasts.

We too are to be reflectors of God's holiness. (See 1 Peter 1:16.) The New Testament words "holy," "saint," and "sanctified" are all derived from a common root in the original Greek language. The basic concept is to be set apart for a specified purpose. As believers, we are set apart from the world to bring glory to God and fulfill His purpose for us.

Neither God nor His plan for man has changed since Creation. God's plan for His people has always been for them to shun false gods and vain use of His name, to honor parents, and to avoid murder, adultery, stealing, and coveting. Nor could anyone past or present ever earn God's acceptance through his own merit. In every age, salvation has always been on the basis of God's grace, received by human faith. It has never been God's will for anyone to perish, but for all people to come to salvation. From cover to cover, the Bible presents a consistent God with a continuous plan of good for people.

7
FINAL EXAM

CAMPING and COVENANT Eras
(Numbers and Deuteronomy)

Maybe you've asked these questions before: If God is all-powerful, why doesn't He just *make* us follow Him? Can't He control us so that we automatically love and serve Him?

Sure, God could program us to do right. But who wants to be loved by a robot? Love has no meaning unless choice is involved.

Wouldn't it be sad if I had to come home each day, find where I parked my wife Karen, put a key in her back, and wind her up to get a mechanical-sounding recording, "I love you. I love you. I love you." Yuk!

Instead, I come home to a person who doesn't *have*

to love me. Karen knows all about my faults and failings, but for her own reasons she chooses to love me anyway.

True Love

Knowing is a key to loving. It's just not possible to *really* love a person you don't know well. When a guy on a blind date expresses his love to a girl he's known for an hour, is that love or hormones at work? True love (the kind the Creator shares) is a choice based on knowledge.

That's what these early books of the Bible are all about: helping people understand what God is like so they can make an intelligent choice to know, love, and serve Him.

In what Bible book does God first tell anyone that He loves him or her? You don't find that happening until the fifth book—Deuteronomy. Does this mean God didn't love Adam, Eve, Noah, Abraham, or Moses? No. We can tell by His actions that He *did* love these and other people.

In what Bible book does God first command anyone to love Him? Once again, it is Deuteronomy. "Love the Lord your God with all your heart and with all your soul and with all your strength (Deuteronomy 6:5). In Genesis through Numbers, God was giving people an opportunity to find out what He is like. Only later does God expect people to *choose* to love Him.

Testing after Teaching

One of God's observable patterns is to teach His people, then test them on what they have learned by giving them choices. Actually, God gives "true-false" tests to see if His people will be true or false to Him. One such test of the Israelites is recorded in Numbers 13—14.

After nearly two years of receiving revelation at Sinai, the Hebrew mob was counted and organized for an orderly move to their Promised Land. "Numbering the Hebrews" is my three-word summary for the Book of Numbers, since there is a census at the beginning and near the ending of the book with wilderness wandering between. The *CAMPING* era tells the story of Israel's movements from Sinai to the Jordan River.

During the *CAMPING* era, the Israelites turned a two-week journey into a 40-year march. What happened? In their unbelief toward God, they failed their final exam on what they had been taught at the Sinai school.

In the face of every evidence imaginable, the

Hebrews voted not to trust God to give them the land. They mistakenly thought the Promised Land would be handed to them on a silver platter! So they wandered in the wilderness for the next 40 years until the entire group of unbelievers died.

The issue which determined a generation's destiny arose on the southern end of the Promised Land at an oasis called Kadesh Barnea. There God's people responded to the reports of 12 spies who had been to Canaan. The first report was not very promising. The land was full of fierce fighters—giants who wouldn't hand over the land easily (Numbers 13:26-33).

The older generation had to make the choice: Would they enter Canaan and claim it by faith as a gift from God? Or would they give in to their fears? They gave in. Because they refused to believe God, both the older and the younger generations had to wander in the wilderness for the next 40 years (Numbers 14:20-23). The older generation, bearing the responsibility of the choice at Kadesh, averaged 82 funerals a day for 40 years! God was effectively teaching both generations that the wages of sin is death (Romans 6:23).

See the map on page 80 for some of the events during the *CAMPING* era.

Why did the Israelites have to wander for 40 years? God gave them one year of wandering in the wilderness for each day the spies had spent checking out the land of Canaan (Numbers 14:32-35). God allowed His people plenty of time to think about their lack of faith in the One who had rescued them from Egypt.

Two Who Did It Right

Two spies believed God was able to conquer Canaan. It's interesting that these two—Joshua and Ca-

SCENES FROM THE CAMPING ERA

(Numbered in order)

Try to guess the events before looking at the key.

1. Israelites organize for the march.
2. Fire from God burns rebellious Israelites.
3. Miriam's hand becomes leprous.
4. Twelve spies explore the Promised Land.
5. Most Israelites refuse to believe God.
6. Israelites wander in the wilderness 40 years.
7. Moses strikes a rock in anger to get water.
8. Moses raises bronze serpent on a pole to heal people bitten by snakes.
9. Balaam talks with his donkey.
10. Israel defeats two pagan kings.
11. Moses teaches from Mount Nebo.

SEA OF GALILEE

CANAAN

Jordan River

Mt. Nebo

MOAB

MEDITERRANEAN SEA

Kadesh–Barnea

DEAD SEA

EDOM

R.I.P.   R.I.P.

RED SEA

MIDIAN

Mt. Sinai

leb—have the same initials as the great Leader of our faith, Jesus Christ. Even though Joshua and Caleb were strong in their faith, the people chose not to listen to their report or follow their example of faith.

One of God's great goals for His people in all ages is that they develop faith in Him. An Old Testament turning point in God's relationship with man took place when Abraham "believed the Lord and He credited it to him as righteousness" (Genesis 15:6).

A similar peak was attained in the New Testament when Peter confessed in faith that Jesus is "the Christ, the Son of the living God" (Matthew 16:16). For this act of faith, Jesus highly praised Peter. Our righteous standing before God is His gift, obtained through our faith in Christ's sacrifice for us.

One great principle of Numbers is that God's testing follows God's teaching. And when a test is failed, a loving Heavenly Father takes His unbelieving children into a "divine woodshed" for disciplining. The issue is not punishment, but training. Faith develops by the choices we make. We take in God's teaching with our minds and emotions. But God's teaching is tested in our wills!

God desires that just as we receive Christ as Saviour by faith, so we should walk in newness of life in Him by faith (Colossians 2:6). God is committed to our education when we choose to enroll in His family training school. I believe that we *will* graduate with a degree of faith—if not in this life, certainly in the next. God's discipline does not reveal His displeasure, but His love. (See Hebrews 12:1-12.)

What decision would *you* have made at Kadesh Barnea? Remember, you would have experienced deliverance from Egypt, God's opening of the Red Sea, manna and quail from heaven, water from rocks, and God's two-year revelation at Mount Sinai. Would you be like Joshua and Caleb, who enjoyed God's "best" because they trusted and obeyed their loving Heavenly Father? Joshua and Caleb were the only two of their generation allowed to enter the Promised Land. They "won" it by their faith. Or would you be like the older generation, wandering in a wilderness of your own making because of your unbelief? God's goal is your faith in Him.

We can't blame our parents for any lack of example or spiritual input. We stand responsible for our own choices. Like the younger generation in the wilderness, we can blossom far more beautifully than our parents. Our heritage does not have to determine our habits!

Let's Make a Deal

The new generation numbered almost as many as their fathers when they camped on the east side of the Jordan River and then conquered everything north of Moab. Moses was still the leader and the central figure.

While Israel camped in the plains of Moab, Moses called the congregation to enter into a covenant with Jehovah, an event which served as a climax to the whole Pentateuch (Deuteronomy 5). The Book of Deuteronomy captures the *COVENANT* era for the historical record and our own instruction. See the big picture of this period on page 83.

A covenant is a two-way agreement. In this covenant God was willing to commit Himself to the Hebrew nation if they would choose to be His special people.

The Deuteronomic covenant was not the first such agreement God made with man. He made a covenant with Noah after the great Flood, promising that never again would He send a flood to destroy the earth. Do you remember God's special sign of this promise? (The rainbow—Genesis 9:8-17.)

SCENES FROM DEUTERONOMY

God made His first Hebrew covenant with Abraham, the first Hebrew (Genesis 12:1-3). Circumcision was the special sign of this agreement (Genesis 17:9-14). And of course there was the major Mosaic covenant made at Mount Sinai in the *COMMANDMENTS* era with the generation rescued from Egypt (recorded in Exodus 20—Numbers 10).

The Deuteronomic covenant was not the last covenant between God and man. God later made one with David during the *CROWNS* era (2 Samuel 7) and predicted a new type of covenant through Jeremiah during the *CAPTIVITY* era (Jeremiah 31). Each of God's covenants has its special sign. Discover these two signs for yourself by reading the passages.

The ultimate covenant between God and man would begin with the special sign of a virgin giving birth to a Son (Isaiah 7:14; Matthew 1:20-23) and would be sealed about 32 years later by the blood of Jesus on Calvary (Matthew 27:26-29).

In Deuteronomy, God renewed His Mosaic covenant with the new generation which survived the wilderness death march. Moses preached three messages, reviewing God's basic requirements for His redeemed people. Since Moses was reviewing the same Law given at Sinai, I summarize the Book of Deuteronomy as "Duplicate of Law."

Through Moses, God pleaded for His people to return His love by obeying His Law. After Israel made this solemn covenant with Jehovah, Moses' work was finally finished.

Normally, if a speaker delivered three long sermons such as found in Deuteronomy, the congregation would die. In this case the preacher perished. But only after a mountaintop view of the Promised Land.

Did Moses ever get to enter Canaan? Yes! It happened centuries later, when Moses appeared with Elijah at Christ's transfiguration (Matthew 17:1-3).

Believe It or Not

See if you can uncover these oddities embodied in the Books of Numbers and Deuteronomy:

☐ How did the Israelites move the ark of the Testimony without ever seeing it? (Numbers 4:4-6)

☐ What strange lie detector test was given to a woman suspected of unfaithfulness to her husband? (Numbers 5:11-28)

☐ What vow required total abstinence from haircuts, grapevines, and funerals? (Numbers 6:1-11)

☐ What kind of meat was delivered to Israel in the wilderness, complete with fire? (Numbers 11:31-33)

☐ What woman's hand was made leprous temporarily for speaking against her brother? (Numbers 12:1-15)

☐ What three men and their families were swallowed in an earthquake crevasse because of their rebellion against authority? (Numbers 16:1-33)

☐ Why was Moses not allowed to enter the Promised Land with Joshua? (Numbers 20:1-12)

☐ Who carried on a conversation with his donkey? (Numbers 22:21-41)

☐ What king had a truly king-sized bed (13 feet long and 6 feet wide)? (Deuteronomy 3:11)

Some Things Never Change

The great foundation of the Bible's first five books is the character of God and His plan for people. Those two things never change. God is revealed as always-existing, all-controlling, all-powerful, everywhere present, all-knowing, all-holy, all-righteous, all-truthful, all-loving, and never-changing.

God is complete perfection—without beginning or end. In His basic essence, He never changes. It is His nature to have fellowship with His creatures; He is never withdrawn. He continues to reveal Himself and desires to be received by us. God's moral principles never change. It has always been His will that people love Him first and foremost, and love their neighbors as themselves.

As in the eras of *CAMPING* and *COVENANT*, loving God is a choice we must make—based on good evidence. To neglect or reject God means wandering in a wilderness of unbelief. But to select Him as worthy of our highest love means to confirm a covenant relationship with the eternal One.

What is the daily test of our love for God? Jesus gave two answers to this question: obey His commandments and love one another (John 15:9-17).

8

BEATING THE BAD GUYS

CONQUEST Era (Joshua)

Jeremy sat in the Bible camp auditorium and talked silently to God. "God, You must have planned this week just for me. That speaker was right on. I know I made a commitment to Christ when I was younger. I'm a Christian all right, but am I a disciple? I haven't been a very good one. But now, things will be different. Jesus is going to be Number One in my life. I've had it with my lukewarm version of Christianity. And just to prove it, I'm going to walk down to the altar and shake the preacher's hand."

But within a week after summer Bible camp closed, Jeremy was fighting with his sister and his mom again. "Maybe next time I can be more sincere about giving my life completely to the Lord," he thought.

It's a familiar story. How many Christian teens do you know who ride this spiritual roller coaster? Almost everyone does. I've faced the same problem in my life.

It Takes Two

When I was a teenager I thought for a long time that I could just let go and let God have His way in my life. After a dedication peak, I'd sit back and leave all the driving to Him. Then later I'd wonder why life wasn't working as it ought to. Years later I discovered that I have responsibilities too. I was surprised to learn that the Christian life should be an active cooperation between us and God. We do what we can, then trust God to do all we can't. The difficulty is that we often have to do our small part *first*.

The Old Testament era of *CONQUEST* dramatically illustrates this truth. The Book of Joshua records the Hebrews' conquest (chapters 1—12) and settlement (chapters 13—24) of Canaan, their Promised Land. Distilled to three words, the Book of Joshua is "Judgment on Canaan." Joshua crossed the Jordan about 1406 B.C. and spent the next seven years in war before homesteading the tribes.

At that time the Hebrews' great escape from Egypt with Moses had been in the history texts for 40 years. A covenant had just been made between the Hebrew elders and the Ruler of the Universe. Imagine the Israelites' feelings: Anticipation runs high. The future seems as bright as God's promises. What their fathers gave up by unbelief in the wilderness, the Hebrews were about to inherit. But they would soon realize that close cooperation with their Creator was vital to Operation Canaan's success.

We Can Do It

Joshua learned the principle of cooperation with God
while serving as Moses' right-hand man for 40 years.
He saw Moses hold up his walking stick so God could
part the Red Sea. He watched Moses hit a rock so God
could open a water tap sufficient for 3½ million people.
When Moses held up his hands (with the help of two
people props) God gave Joshua victory in Israel's first
battle with the Amalekites.

The Divine Commander reminded Joshua about this
cooperation principle. God told His newly appointed
Hebrew leader, "Do not let this Book of the Law depart
from your mouth; meditate on it day and night, so that
you may be careful to do everything written in it. Then
you will be prosperous and successful" (Joshua 1:8).

It's no wonder then that we see Joshua in every
chapter of his book doing what he could do and trusting
God to take care of the rest. For example, when two
Hebrew spies ventured into Jericho, God guided them.
When the innkeeper Rahab hid the two foreign scouts
on her Jericho rooftop, God protected them (Joshua
2).

To reach Jericho, Joshua led the people across the
Jordan River on dry ground, and for the second time
God miraculously parted water for His people. But first
the priests had to step into the water while the river was
at flood stage! When they did, God dried up a pathway
20 miles wide. We know this because Joshua carefully
noted the two points where the waters separated
(Joshua 3:14-17).

While the waters were parted the Hebrews set up 24
memorial stones—12 each in the riverbed and on the
bank. They trusted God to later give their children
curiosity about the stones, so future generations would
be reminded of God's power and protection. Only after

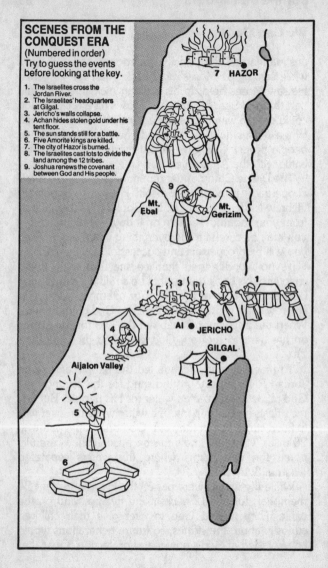

SCENES FROM THE CONQUEST ERA

(Numbered in order)
Try to guess the events before looking at the key.

1. The Israelites cross the Jordan River.
2. The Israelites' headquarters at Gilgal.
3. Jericho's walls collapse.
4. Achan hides stolen gold under his tent floor.
5. The sun stands still for a battle.
6. Five Amorite kings are killed.
7. The city of Hazor is burned.
8. The Israelites cast lots to divide the land among the 12 tribes.
9. Joshua renews the covenant between God and His people.

7 HAZOR

8

9

Mt. Ebal

Mt. Gerizim

3

1

4

AI ● ● JERICHO

GILGAL ●

2

Aijalon Valley

5

6

the priests climbed out of the riverbed did God cause the waters to flow again.

Strange Military Strategies

Once across the Jordan, Israel camped south of Jericho. They conquered the midsection of Canaan first, starting with Jericho. The "strategy" by which Joshua took Jericho is known to every Sunday School student. How many times did the Hebrews march around the city before the Lord knocked the walls down? Thirteen is the right answer (Joshua 6:3-4). But Jericho was the only city they conquered by such a strange maneuver.

The Jericho experience is a reminder that God's work must be done in His way. His people were not just to do what seemed reasonable naturally, but what God revealed supernaturally. In every new situation they had to seek fresh counsel from God.

Have you ever mistakenly thought you could find God's will for life and not have to search anymore? I fell into that trap, thinking a call to the pastorate meant settling in for life! Being sensitive to the Spirit's leading is a lifetime process.

Back to the Battle

Defeat came to the Hebrews next, at Ai, because they violated God's plan twice. First, Achan kept part of the Jericho loot, which belonged to God (Joshua 7:1). Second, Joshua did not seek God's strategy for capturing Ai. The Hebrews decided on their own how they thought it should best be accomplished. Only after their resounding defeat did they ask God how *He* wanted them to capture this town. After they dealt with Achan's sin and sought the Lord, He told them how to take Ai, using an ambush technique. As long as Joshua held up his spear, God gave the Israelites victory over the men of Ai (Joshua 8:18-26).

Not seeking God's will again allowed the Israelites to be tricked into a treaty with the Gibeonites (Joshua 9). This treaty prevented them from getting rid of the wicked Canaanites in that area, as God had commanded.

When God's people sought and followed God's will, things went according to the divine plan, with God's help. In one battle Joshua prayed for the sun to "stand still," and God lengthened the day until victory was complete.

By conquering Jericho and the central section of the land, the Israelites had effectively divided Canaan in half. This made it easier for them to conquer the rest of the Promised Land—first the southern sector and then the north.

The Book of Joshua is filled with stories of battle and bloodshed. Was all that violence necessary? We must realize that God used the Hebrews as His tools of judgment on a polluted people who were nearly ripe for extermination 600 years earlier, in the days of Abraham (Genesis 15:16). The Canaanites had received plenty of warning and time to change their ways. Read about the terrible practices of the pagan Baal religion, and you will realize Joshua was removing a malignant cancer from the human race.

Lots for Lots

In the second half of Joshua's book (13—24), the Israelites divided up the land by lot, to determine where each tribe would settle. Again the principle of human-

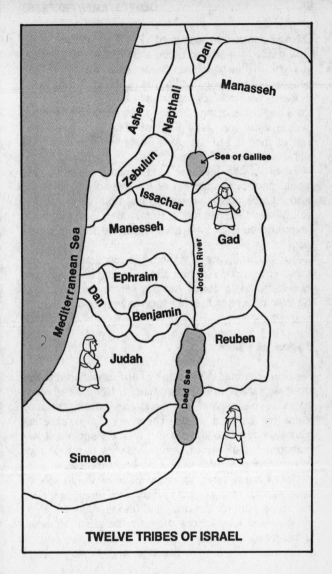

TWELVE TRIBES OF ISRAEL

Divine cooperation was used. The Hebrews cast lots; God guided where each tribe should dwell in Canaan.

Think of the squabbles twelve tribes of 3½ million people would have dividing up Canaan if they used modern methods of committee and caucus. They would still be arguing about it! (Yes, they had as many people at the end of the 40 years of wilderness wanderings as they did at the start. Compare Numbers 1:46 with Numbers 26:51.)

To avoid bad feelings, God made it clear that He would control the casting of the lots to distribute the lands. Once again we see an example of the supernatural way God can guide. Remember, God's work, to be harmonious and effective, must be done in God's way!

Ask yourself, are you doing today what God has called you to do? Are you also following His leading in *how* it should be done? Are you sensitive to and seeking new directions that He may have for you today?

Pages of Places

We don't read far in the Book of Joshua without realizing that place names are prominent. Remove all references to places and the Scriptures would certainly shrink in size and sense! There are 1,551 separate places woven into the Word of God—and most are mentioned many times. Jerusalem wins the trophy for "most mentions" with over 2,500 occurrences.

Places are referred to in the Bible as they relate to people, with one exception. Hell was never prepared for people, but for the devil and his fallen angels. People go there who ignore or reject the salvation Jesus Christ freely offers.

Christianity is both a historical and a geographical

faith. God has dared to fill His written record with names of people and places which can be checked on by history and archeology. One of the first things we notice about the "sacred" books of the great man-made world religions is an emphasis on philosophy and an absence of people and places.

A totally inspired and authoritative Bible means every word is significant and worthy of study. This includes people and places too! Perhaps many of us in this New Testament Age still believe in "the passover principle." We come to strange words and names in the Bible and "pass over" them, hoping they will go away! A Bible dictionary or encyclopedia is a valuable resource. Keep one close at hand to look up names of places you come across in Scripture studies. And try referring regularly to Bible maps to better understand where things happened in the lands of the Bible. It will make God's whole picture clearer!

God, What Are You Doing?

The Hebrew history books—Genesis through Esther—explain how God's character and plan for man should have worked out in the story of one nation.

The Hebrew people had been given a message from God. They were supposed to demonstrate this message for humanity. God's precepts were to be their practice; His Law their life. By following Him, they would make the world thirsty for the quality of life the one true God could produce in people. God was not "playing favorites" with the Hebrews, but only using them to provoke other people to an active faith in Him.

Did the method work? Yes and no. While Israel walked in faith and obedience to God, it worked well. But when the people of Israel chose to go their way in unbelief and rebellion, the plan flopped!

God is such a careful Teacher that He did not allow the foreign nations to get the wrong idea from His people. These nations could clearly see God blessing Israel's faith and obedience. They also saw God disciplining His people for lack of faith and obedience. In the same way, people can observe God at work in our lives today. We who belong to God *will* be witnesses. Our only choice is what *kind* of witnesses we'll be.

The rest of the Old Testament historical record relates Israel's "roller coaster" spiritual state as they kept reaching for and falling from faith and obedience. Sounds like modern Christian experience, doesn't it?

The Christian life doesn't *have* to be that way—two steps back for every one step forward. God's provision for complete victory is always available; all we have to do is make use of it. We can each learn a lesson from General Joshua, "Success in life requires our cooperation with God."

9

CYCLING DOWNHILL

CYCLES Era (Judges 1—1 Samuel 8)

The philosopher Hegel once said that the only thing we learn from history is that we don't learn anything from history. In other words, those who ignore the past are condemned to repeat it.

Because it is so important to learn from the past, God has recorded in Scripture people's successes as well as their failures. God wants us to learn from history—especially "His story." If we follow the examples and instructions of Scripture, we won't have to learn the ways of God only through personal experience and our own failures. We can see where others went wrong. In the New Testament, the Apostle Paul wrote about the importance of learning from the Israelites' mistakes:

"These things happened to them as examples and were written down as warnings for us" (1 Corinthians 10:1-14).

The Book of Judges and the first eight chapters of 1 Samuel record seven cycles which the Hebrews kept repeating. Apparently they had a problem with learning from the past. I call this section the era of *CYCLES*—sin cycles.

Pay close attention when you read Judges, and see if you don't agree that it seems very modern. With an update of personalities and places, the Book of Judges could pass as a contemporary critique of our country.

The keys to Judges hang on both doors to the book. At the front door we are told a new generation arose that knew neither Joshua nor Jehovah. At the end of the book we learn that everyone did what he wanted to

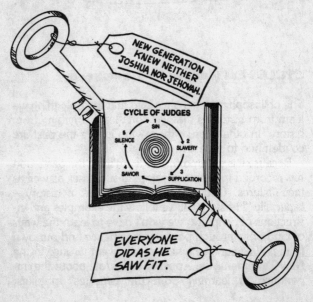

do. No one cared about God or His laws.

During the time of Judges, Israel was moving from theocracy (God's direct rule) to monarchy (God's indirect rule through kings). Seven times Israel spun through a cycle of sin, servitude, supplication, salvation, and silence—only to sin again. A suitable three-word summary of Judges is "Jewish Sin Cycles."

The period of the Judges covers about 350 years. It begins with Joshua, about 1400 B.C., and ends with the crowning of Saul in 1050 B.C. Deborah, Barak, Gideon, Jephthah, and Samson were some of the more familiar national heroes called judges.

Here We Go Again

The first of the sin cycles began before Israel's first judge took over. It started with sin. "The Israelites did evil in the eyes of the Lord; they forgot the Lord their God, and served the Baals and the Asherahs" (Judges 3:7).

☐ Step two: servitude—"The anger of the Lord burned against Israel so that He sold them into the hands of Cushan-Rishathaim king of Aram Naharaim, to whom the Israelites were subject for eight years" (Judges 3:8).

☐ Step three: supplication—"[The Israelites] cried out to the Lord" (Judges 3:9).

☐ Step four: salvation—"[The Lord] raised up for them a deliverer, Othniel . . . who saved them. The Spirit of the Lord came upon him, so that he became Israel's judge and went to war" (Judges 3:9-10).

☐ Step five: silence—"And the Israelites served the Lord happily ever after" (Hall reversed version). I wish it said that—but the next verse tells of a strange silence that settled over the land for 40 years (Judges 3:11). And then we read, "Once again the Israelites did evil in

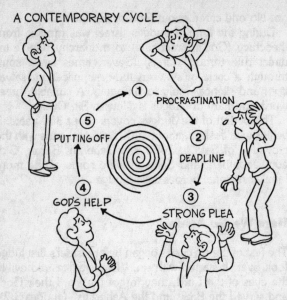

A CONTEMPORARY CYCLE

① PROCRASTINATION

⑤ PUTTING OFF

② DEADLINE

④ GOD'S HELP

③ STRONG PLEA

the eyes of the Lord" (Judges 3:12). The Israelites were starting the second of their seven sin cycles.

The sin cycle is not just a special problem of God's Old Testament people. It unfortunately occurs all too often today in the personal experiences of God's New Testament believers.

For example, let's look at the sin we call procrastination. We may put off doing things we know God wants us to do. We become slaves to deadlines we can't seem to meet. We beg God for help and promise to do better next time. God may choose to bail us out—saving us from problems we bring on ourselves. Or He may allow us to learn some lessons through failure. As we continue the cycle, do we keep the commitments we made when in trouble? Or does a silence settle over our communication with God? Often we do return to our old ways, and before long, the cycle is repeated.

Try to recall mistakes and errors you've made more than once in life. Are you trying to learn from the experiences of Bible personalities? Are you also profiting from shared experiences of other believers you know? Are you growing spiritually by letting God break your own sin cycles? Remember, if we don't learn from the past, we will most likely repeat it.

Meet the Judge

There were fourteen judges who ruled the Hebrews in Canaan between General Joshua and King Saul. Twelve ruled during the Book of Judges time period and two ruled in 1 Samuel. How many of the judges can you name? Do the names Tola, Jair, Ehud, or Shamgar ring any bells? These were not judges like we think of judges—sitting at a high desk and making decisions. They were leaders, heroes, men of action.

Test your "judge-ment." Which judge:

☐ Was the only person in the Bible said to be left-handed?

☐ Used a fleece to learn God's will?

☐ Made a rash vow to sacrifice to God whoever came out of his house first—and it happened to be his daughter?

☐ Anointed both Saul and David as kings?

☐ Struck down 600 enemy troops with an oxgoad?

☐ Was a woman judge, a prophetess, and poet?

☐ Had long hair, great strength, and was preoccupied with women?

☐ Killed 69 of his half-brothers to become the next ruler?

☐ Was a priest-judge when the tabernacle ark was captured by the Philistines?

Find the answers in this brief look at the judges as they appeared on history's stage.

1. **OTHNIEL**, nephew and son-in-law to Caleb (the spy), delivered Israel from Mesopotamian oppression in sin cycle one (Judges 3:1-11).

2. **EHUD** used his left-handedness to slip a surprise dagger into King Eglon of Moab, delivering Israel in sin cycle two (Judges 3:12-30).

3. **SHAMGAR** used an oxgoad to kill 600 Philistines in sin cycle three (Judges 3:31).

4. **DEBORAH** was the only woman judge. **Barak**, who was her chief general, wouldn't go to battle unless Deborah came also. Some count fifteen judges by separating these two. Actually, a woman named Jael gets credit for killing the leader of the Canaanite forces in sin cycle four. Read the account in Judges 4 and see if you think the expression "hitting the nail on the head" originated here.

You Can't Miss It

5. **GIDEON** is one of only four judges on whom the Holy Spirit is said to have come. Othniel, Jephthah, and Samson were the others. Gideon was called into service during sin cycle five. He wanted a visible sign from God that he was really supposed to save Israel from the Midianites. So Gideon asked God to dampen his fleece (a woolly sheepskin) while the surrounding ground remained dry. That wasn't enough of a sign for Gideon. He wanted to see if God would reverse the process. The next morning Gideon sloshed through the thick dew and picked up a perfectly dry and dusty sheepskin from the otherwise wet ground.

How patient the Lord is with His people! To me, Gideon's requests were in the same league as the teen who asked the Lord to let two of the four tires be flat on his car overnight in the garage if he was not to date a certain girl. That done, he asked God to reverse it the next night and make the other two tires and the spare flat! But God graciously gave Gideon his desired signs, and has been known to do similarly since (though He has no obligation to do so).

God decreased Gideon's army from 32,000 to 300. (Read about the strange way the 300 fighters were chosen in Judges 7.) God sent Gideon and the 300 to battle with trumpets, pitchers, and torches. Because of their obedience, God gave victory.

After Gideon's graduation to glory, his illegitimate son Abimelech killed 69 of Gideon's 70 sons to seize power in Israel. But a millstone, pushed by a woman from an upper story, crushed Abimelech's cruel career (not to mention his crown).

6. **TOLA** and

7. **JAIR** ruled 50 years in Israel. Children and donkeys were Jair's claim to fame (Judges 10:3-5).

8. **JEPHTHAH** defeated the Ammonites (descendants of Abraham's nephew Lot—see Genesis 19:30-38) in sin cycle six. But the sweet smell of success suddenly turned sour as his daughter ran from his house to welcome him home. He had expected an animal would run to him first (see Judges 11:29-40).

9. **IBZAN**,

10. **ELON**, and

11. **ABDON** filled 25 peaceful years with children and donkeys also (see Judges 12:8-15).

Strike Three—You're Out

12. **SAMSON** was one of three judges given the most copy space by the Heavenly Editor (the Deborah-Barak

team and Gideon are the others). Sin cycle seven (oppression by the Philistines) continued through the next two judges and into the reigns of the first two kings of the Israelites. Do you remember the giant Goliath's nationality and whose forces killed King Saul? The answer is Philistine in both cases.

The lesson to be learned from Samson is not that growing long hair makes a guy macho. Read Samson's life story carefully (Judges 13—16) in the light of his three Nazirite vow obligations. (Check Numbers 6:1-21 for the scoop on the vow.) You'll find Samson's haircut by barber Delilah meant he was breaking the third part of his vow. Samson had broken the other two parts previously. He lost his strength through his own carelessness in ignoring his duty to God.

Satan likes to hide the long-range consequences of

sin, but God's Word clearly connects them. Samson paid a high price for his sin. He was captured, blinded by his enemies, and humiliated—forced to do the work of an ox. Samson is an illustration (appropriate but not beautiful) of the truthfulness of Ecclesiastes 5:4-5, "When you make a vow to God, do not delay in fulfilling it. He has no pleasure in fools; fulfill your vow. It is better not to vow than to make a vow and not fulfill it."

By the way, from what common disease did Samson die? Fallen arches! In the end, with his hair grown back, Samson's strength returned. He pulled down the arches of the Philistine banquet hall, killing more of the enemy in his suicide than he had done previously.

13. **ELI** was the priest-judge into whose care Hannah committed her son Samuel as an intern. During his time, the Philistines continued to oppress Israel. They captured the tabernacle ark—the most holy piece of furniture which held the two stone tablets of Law, Aaron's rod that budded, and a jar of manna. Eli literally died when he heard that bad news (1 Samuel 4:17-18).

The Philistines soon discovered the ark brought only trouble and disease to those who weren't meant to have it. So Israel's enemy put the sacred chest on a cart pulled by two unbroken oxen, who took it straight back to its proper home (1 Samuel 5—6).

We Want a King

14. **SAMUEL**, the first recorded circuit rider preacher and governor (1 Samuel 7:16-17), was the last of the fourteen judges. He finally gave in to the people's pleas for a king by anointing Saul.

Samuel's life ended in sorrow, because he was rejected by the people he had served all his career. Samuel's sons were not godly men, and the people feared they might become the next rulers. "But his sons did not walk in his ways. They turned aside after dishonest gain and accepted bribes and perverted justice" (1 Samuel 8:3).

Samuel's wounded spirit bitterly flavors his farewell state-of-the-union address (chapter 12). Had Samuel been too busy in the kingdom for the welfare of his family? Did he try hard enough to influence the people of Israel? We wonder what regrets old Samuel had—looking back on a life that started out with great promise and ended with rejection by family and followers.

It is dangerous to rest on a good start. Our heritage may offer us a good foundation. Past victories and accomplishments may make good building blocks for life. But we can't rest on our laurels, for our "enemy, the devil, prowls about like a roaring lion, looking for someone to devour" (1 Peter 5:8). We must continually seek the face of the Lord daily for new victories and a new supply of strength in our walk with Him. We must ever humble ourselves under the mighty hand of God, so that He may lift us up at the proper time (1 Peter 5:6).

Love Story

What happens in a society when each person thinks he or she is above the law? Read for yourself (but only when you have a strong stomach) the toll that apostasy (spiritual rebellion), immorality, and anarchy (lawlessness) take on individuals as well as their nation. (See Judges 17—21.)

Do we have to go down the tubes just because our society does? Can a person stay pure when everyone else isn't? Let Ruth answer these two questions through her story of faith and devotion.

Ruth's is a classic love story of tragedy turned to

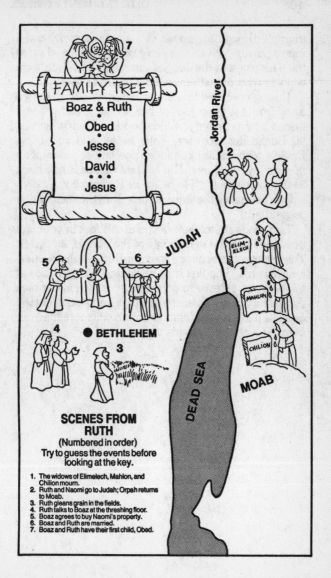

FAMILY TREE

Boaz & Ruth
•
Obed
•
Jesse
•
David
•••
Jesus

Jordan River

JUDAH

• BETHLEHEM

ELIM-ELECH

MAHLON

CHILION

DEAD SEA

MOAB

SCENES FROM RUTH

(Numbered in order)
Try to guess the events before looking at the key.

1. The widows of Elimelech, Mahlon, and Chilion mourn.
2. Ruth and Naomi go to Judah; Orpah returns to Moab.
3. Ruth gleans grain in the fields.
4. Ruth talks to Boaz at the threshing floor.
5. Boaz agrees to buy Naomi's property.
6. Boaz and Ruth are married.
7. Boaz and Ruth have their first child, Obed.

triumph through the power of a woman's purity and a man's pursuing love. This story is a shining jewel set in the dark stone of the Judges' era. Boaz and Ruth were winners who did what was right in God's eyes.

Through her love for her mother-in-law, Ruth turned away from the false gods of her people. Later she was rescued from poverty, widowhood, and childlessness by Boaz's love for her. Their union and son (King David's grandfather) continued the line of redemption that led toward Christ. This is why I reduce Ruth's book to the three words, "Romance of Redemption."

Can you recall the story of Ruth from the sketches on page 107?

Two roads stretch before you at this fork in your life: one leads into the ugly jungle of the Judges sin cycles. The other is the beautiful route of Ruth's righteousness and rewards. The first is characterized by ignorance of the past and a desire to do whatever is right in our own eyes. The latter is characterized by a knowledge of God and His plans and a desire to do His will more than our own. The choice of roads is up to you.

10

WE THREE KINGS

CROWNS Era (1 Samuel 9—1 Kings 11; 1 Chronicles 1—2 Chronicles 9)

Sue was arguing with her best friend. "I just can't accept your brand of religion. It's too easy. It turns people into hypocrites. You say God forgives all your sin: past, present, and future. If that's really true, then you can live as you please and still claim to be a Christian." If you were Sue's friend, how would you respond? How would you answer Sue's objection to the Christian way because it seems to promote a lifestyle of doing whatever you want?

We can discover a good answer within the life of King David. He was the middle king of the first 120 years of the *CROWNS* era. But before we look at David's life, let's set the historical stage.

The Kingdom Fork

We're near the top of our four symbols in Canaan. Can you list them? They are the sword for *CONQUEST*, gavel for *CYCLES*, crown for *CROWNS*, and split crown for *CHASM*. (See map, page 26.)

Next to the prophets, most people find the kings the most confusing section of the Scriptures. This section begins with the first king, Saul (1 Samuel 9), and continues until the captivities described in 2 Chronicles and 2 Kings.

There are six historical books about the Hebrew kingdom, meaning the time in the Old Testament when the Hebrews were governed by their own chosen kings. These six books consist of three sets of "twins": the Samuels, the Kings, and the Chronicles.

THE KINGDOM FORK

SAUL
1 Samuel 9—31

SOLOMON
1 Kings 1—11

DAVID
2 Samuel

120 Years

KINGDOM SPLIT
930 B.C.

ISRAEL
208 Years

ASSYRIAN CAPTIVITY

CHASM
1 Kings 12—2 Kings 16

JUDAH
344 Years

BABYLONIAN CAPTIVITY

It may help you form a clearer image of this era by picturing the Old Testament kingdom as a long tuning fork. The handle of our kingdom tuning fork represents one whole Bible book (2 Samuel) flanked by parts of two others (1 Samuel 9—31 and 1 Kings 1—11). Each Scripture segment tells the story of one Hebrew king ruling over the united tribes of Israel. In 1 Samuel, Saul serves as the first king, setting a poor example for the rest to follow. In 2 Samuel, David is usually the man after God's own heart (Acts 13:22). In 1 Kings 1—11, Solomon serves God for a season, then divides his loyalties among the gods of his many pagan wives. The "united tribes" segment, which I have called the *CROWNS* era, is the subject of this chapter.

For our memory convenience, Saul, David, and Solomon (I remember them as "SDS") each ruled for 40 years. This reminds us of Moses, whose 120-year life was divided in three 40-year segments: prince, shepherd, and prophet.

Looking at the fork picture, you might guess that there are two kingdoms in the last half of 1 Kings and during 2 Kings. These 1½ books describe the 19 kings which followed Solomon in each of the two kingdoms. (The South even did one better than the North by adding a queen.) This is the "divided tribes" of Israel period during the *CHASM* era—the subject of the next chapter. The Northern Kingdom, called Israel, was conquered by Assyria in 722 B.C. Babylon took Judah, the Southern Kingdom, in 586 B.C.

Saul—Sidetracked by the Green-eyed Monster

Two men dominate the Book of 1 Samuel. Samuel was the last of the fourteen judges and gave in to the peoples' call for a king by anointing Saul. King Saul's slide into sin and his jealous pursuit of David (destined to be the next king) was in total contrast to godly Samuel. A suitable three-word summary of 1 Samuel is "Samuel and Saul."

Saul is described as "a choice and handsome man," taller than anyone else in Israel. His father, Kish, was a mighty man of courage and apparently wealthy (1 Samuel 9:1-3). After Saul was privately anointed and taught by Samuel, he took over as king during a national emergency (1 Samuel 11). As a new king, Saul won further acclaim by great victories over the Ammonites and the Philistines early in his reign.

There is some humor in 1 Samuel 10 too. Picture all Israel gathered to inaugurate their first king. When it's time to take the oath of office, the king has mysteriously disappeared. "But he was just here a minute ago." So everyone scrambles to find Saul. Finally he turns up— hiding in the luggage pile!

Even though he started well, Saul's life ended in a depressed suicide on the battlefield (1 Samuel 31). His downfall began when he substituted his own reasoning for God's clear commands which came through Samuel (1 Samuel 13). When confronted with his sin, Saul didn't repent, but rather offered more excuses. It's not hard to find or make up good reasons to sin! Things went from bad to worse for Saul, until finally his kingdom was taken away from him and given to David (1 Samuel 16:1).

Something snapped in Saul's head when he heard people comparing one of his soldiers, David, to the king: "Saul has slain his thousands, and David his tens of thousands" (1 Samuel 18:7). Saul spent the rest of his life insanely jealous of David, seeking to kill him (1 Samuel 18—30). The green-eyed monster of jealousy devoured him.

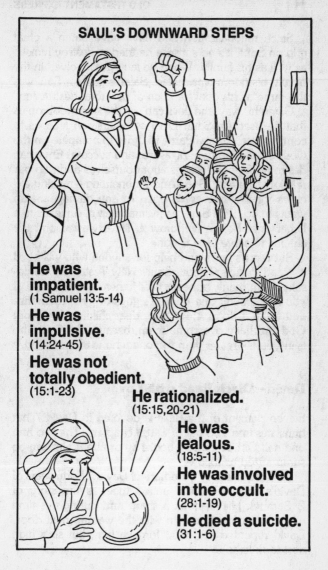

SAUL'S DOWNWARD STEPS

He was impatient.
(1 Samuel 13:5-14)

He was impulsive.
(14:24-45)

He was not totally obedient.
(15:1-23)

He rationalized.
(15:15,20-21)

He was jealous.
(18:5-11)

He was involved in the occult.
(28:1-19)

He died a suicide.
(31:1-6)

Since rationalization and envy gave Satan a great grip on Saul, it's no surprise he tried to destroy himself as well as his family. When he later got involved in the occult, his doom was sealed. Satan's goal for Saul was the same as his goal for each of us—total destruction.

Given his way, the devil can use the same tools on us that he used on Saul. Envy of others can lead us to compromise our standards in order to compete on the world's level for love, pleasure, and success. Envy can destroy our good feelings about ourselves and ruin our relationships with God. And rationalizing—making excuses for sin—leaves us open to any damage Satan wants to do. Like Saul, each small step of sin leads to a larger one. Before we know it, life is wasted and the chance to serve God is gone.

But there's hope and help for anyone who will heed it. Read in Acts 9 about Saul's New Testament namesake—a humanly hopeless case if there ever was one. If you are already one of God's guys or girls, memorize and claim 1 John 4:4, "You, dear children, are from God and have overcome them, because the One who is in you is greater than the one who is in the world."

David—Disciplined with Love

Eleven percent of the Bible is devoted to David. That translates into 126 out of 1,189 chapters. The two and one half Old Testament books by or about him can be summarized as follows:

   ☐ **2 Samuel**—"Summary of David." Forty years of David's reign over the united tribes is the story of 2 Samuel. His life took a sharp turn during this time when he stepped into sin with the woman next door. David repented and God forgave him, but sin's high cost took its toll.

☐ **1 Chronicles**—"Commentary on Samuel." First Chronicles is God's commentary on the same story as 2 Samuel. The divine Editor's front-page story is about David's preparations to build God a temple, making it easier for Solomon to carry out the huge task. Interviews with key people in the kingdom also get heavy coverage in 1 Chronicles.

☐ **Psalms**—"Praises and Petitions." David wrote half of the psalms we find in the Bible—75 of 150. The psalms' opening notes identify 73 as his, and the New Testament quotes two unidentified psalms as David's (Psalm 2 in Acts 4:25 and Psalm 95 in Hebrews 4:7).

Psalms individually and collectively divide about equally into praise for God's character and works and for petition that He would work more! I feel much at home in David's psalms especially; they are a beautiful blend of the human and the Divine balanced in a believer. In one breath David was eager for God to take more swift action against his persecutors. In the next breath David was full of gratitude and confidence for what God was doing and would do on his behalf. One lesson we can learn from David is to be aware of the balance in our prayer life between "Thank You/I adore You" and "Help me/give me."

Two Lifestyles

Throughout all of 2 Samuel, there is only one king of the Hebrews. He is David, called a man after God's own heart (1 Samuel 13:14). But David evidenced two distinct lifestyles, divided by his relationship with his neighbor Bathsheba.

In chapters 1—10 of 2 Samuel, everything was going great for David. His kingdom was expanding to its greatest size ever—from Egypt to the Euphrates. Israel was fast becoming the major world power. Wealth and tribute flowed into Jerusalem, David's new capital and worship center.

The rest of 2 Samuel provides a sharp contrast. Foreign enemies began to take back their lands from Israel. David's own children rebelled against his authority and chased him out of the capital. His wives and concubines were captured and claimed by one of his sons. For the rest of David's life there was incest and bloodshed within his family.

The difference between David's lifestyle of rejoicing and regret came as a result of one blatant incident of sin. David's troubles deepened the more he tried to cover his dirty tracks.

After the Prophet Nathan confronted King David with his terrible sin, David showed he was still a man after God's own heart by his remorse and repentance (see Psalms 32; 51). But God dramatically demonstrated (2 Samuel 12) that there are consequences of *forgiven* sin! Nathan assured David of God's forgiveness, but also announced: (1) the child born of the illicit union would die, (2) the sword would never depart from David's house, and (3) his women would be taken publicly from him. In 2 Samuel 13—24 we can see the fulfillment of all these prophecies.

Satan is a master at hiding the long-term results of a moment of sinful rebellion against heaven's throne. God won't allow His people to live a lifestyle that suggests sin can freely and easily be forgiven because grace comes cheap. This attitude shows complete disrespect for the Cross of Calvary. The free gift of grace cost God the life of His Son. If there were any other way a holy God could forgive sin, other than having His perfect Son nailed to a cross at the hands of sinners, He would have done it. But that is the only way a God of holiness could satisfy His love toward us. And, just as with

David, God will not let His people go undisciplined for their sins.

God allows us to choose to do good or evil, but He also lets us live with the results of our choices. If I robbed a bank and truly repented, God would forgive me. But I would still have to pay my debt to society through repayment and/or imprisonment! I could smoke for years, but prayer wouldn't necessarily keep the lung cancer away. Just as certain vices have their diseases, so all forgiven sin has its consequences.

Does this mean God holds grudges and only reluctantly forgives? Not at all! We shouldn't confuse His discipline with His displeasure. God, the caring Creator, disciplines everyone He loves (Proverbs 3:11-12). God is a good parent to those He has adopted spiritually in Christ. He gives clear instruction and tests our understanding of it. When God's discipline must be administered, it is always followed by a reminder of His love.

Look how God encouraged David and Bathsheba. Though their baby died, David understood that the departed one had gone to heaven (2 Samuel 12:23). David and Bathsheba's next child was Solomon, whom God chose to be the next king of Israel. Solomon also became the wisest and wealthiest king ever. Note the Lord's love for the new baby boy (2 Samuel 12:24-25). God even gave him the nickname Jedidiah, meaning "beloved of the Lord."

And in God's editorial on the life of David in 1 Chronicles one of David's sins is not even mentioned or hinted at. The entire illicit incident with Bathsheba is missing from that sacred record. God forgives and somehow forgets forgiven sin.

How else could God have reaffirmed His love to His two children who were living out the consequences of forgiven sin? Here is a true *antinomy* — two equally weighty truths which seem opposite. On the one hand, God through Christ removes our sins as far from us as east is from the west (Psalm 103:12, a psalm of David). On the other hand, God allows us to live with results of forgiven sin as an object lesson to our world (2 Samuel 12:13-14).

Solomon—Split Loyalties

Since about 6 percent of the Scripture is by or about Solomon (68 out of 1,189 chapters), he too must be in the Bible's "big league." These chapters could be condensed as follows:

☐ **1 Kings**—"Kingdom Is Divided." Solomon inherited his father David's kingdom and began a building program which included the temple in Jerusalem. God's beautiful temple rivaled any wonder of the ancient world. However, it was costly to build and when the people requested tax reduction, they were turned down by Solomon's son. Ten tribes separated from the united tribes of Israel (1 Kings 12), and as a result there were two Hebrew kings in separate capitals. The North was called Israel; the South was called Judah.

☐ **2 Chronicles**—"Commentary on Kings." The divine Editor's second edition tells of Judah, the Southern Kingdom. It begins with Solomon's reign and ends with slavery to Babylon. In this account, each king is scored on the Heavenly Opinion Poll based on the standard: David's heart for God. In the end, paying the price for disobeying God, the people are carted into captivity by Babylon. However, 2 Chronicles concludes with a promising assurance of return home after 70 years.

Second Chronicles is essentially the same as 1 and 2 Kings. If you want to be technically correct,

2 Chronicles would start with Solomon's third of the single handle and continue only over the bottom bar of the kingdom fork to Babylon. (See Kingdom Fork, page 110.) Chronicles traces the line of kings only through Judah, the line of promise eventually leading to the King of kings, Christ. Solomon's story is in 2 Chronicles 1—9.

Solomon's life can be summarized by the three books of experience he wrote, taking them in their *SPE*cial chronological order. The *S*ong stems from Solomon's youthful years, *P*roverbs from the mature years of his kingship as he used God's gifts, and *E*cclesiastes was written later in life as he pondered his squandered senior-citizen years.

☐ **Song of Songs**—"Sex in Marriage." It used to be that Jewish males couldn't read this quasi sex-in-

marriage manual until they were 30 years old! Here is the Creator's corrective for distortions of what He designed to be a delight in its proper context, marriage. Through this ancient poem we are reminded of our wise and wonderful God, who designed us male and female and provided such a beautiful bond of love.

☐ **Proverbs**—"Prudence in Life." In the 915 verses of Proverbs are a wealth of practical guidelines for a wise and profitable life. In Proverbs you'll find a fairly equal number of do's and don'ts. The wisdom we pick up in Proverbs is more than clever sayings. Here wisdom means the skill of living life as the Creator designed it. Success in living can be found packaged in the compact capsules of Proverbs.

Since Solomon wrote about 3,000 proverbs (1 Kings 4:32), get with him on a cloud in the next life and ask for the other 2,085 which didn't get preserved for us now. Also ask him to sing some of his 1,005 songs.

☐ **Ecclesiastes**—"Emptiness in Life." Hindsight always seems clearer than foresight. It's easier to look back and see our mistakes, learning from life's experiences. Such was the case of Solomon's Ecclesiastes. This book reads like a catalog of what many people today would consider necessary for success in life: wisdom, pleasure, wealth, work, friends, popularity, religion, marriage, children, and status. Solomon had tried them all and declared them all to be empty.

While nothing on the list is necessarily wrong—neither are any of these catalog items completely satisfying as the major purpose of life. To focus our lives on any of these earthly things is like grasping for a soap bubble. As we grasp, we experience the law of diminishing returns! Our greater efforts only bring decreased satisfaction. Solomon's conclusion is, "Fear God and keep His commandments, for this is the whole duty of man" (Ecclesiastes 12:13).

The Voices of Experience

The four experience books—Psalms through Song of Songs—penned during the *CROWNS* period are timeless. Young people turn to them time and again because these books deal with the deep needs in every human heart. (Remember the fifth Old Testament experience book, Job, took place during the *CLAN* period of Genesis 12—50.) Each of the four experience books deals with critical questions of life:

☐ **Psalms**—How can we worship God in a wicked world? How do we stay pure when persecuted?

☐ **Proverbs**—Where can we find wisdom for the practical problems of everyday life?

☐ **Ecclesiastes**—What really makes life worth living after all?

☐ **Song of Songs**—What is God's view of sex?

Note the proper progression in how the five experience books are placed in our Bibles. Suffering and circumstances beyond our control should cause us to turn to an all-powerful God (Job) and worship Him alone (Psalms). The fear and worship of God is the beginning and source of wisdom for daily living (Proverbs). Two major areas in which we need to apply God's wisdom are purpose in life (Ecclesiastes) and a proper relationship to the opposite sex (Song of Songs).

Saul's, David's, and Solomon's lives serve to warn us to walk closely with God each day. We can't rest on our past successes with God. Neither can we sit and dream of what God will do for us. No matter how great our start down the right path, we must see the race through to its proper finish.

11

SPLITS AND SPLINTERS

CHASM era (1 Kings 12—2 Kings 16; 2 Chronicles 10—28)

Samuel had warned the people: Persistence in placing a human king in power over the Hebrews would carry a hefty price tag. Their best young men would be sent to battle, risking death or injury. Their choice young women would become part of the king's harem. Taxes would become so high to pay for the king's programs and building projects that eventually the people would have to rebel.

Besides, their whole motivation was wrong. Israel wanted a human king to be like the nations around them—the Hittites, Moabites, Canaanites, and other parasites. In the process they were rejecting their Heavenly King, God.

Problems, Problems, Problems

The first three kings of the *CROWNS* era made some progress for the Israelites, but they mainly left behind a pile of problems.

Solomon was followed by his son, Rehoboam. Soon after Rehoboam took power, a delegation from the ten Northern Tribes asked for a tax cut (1 Kings 12:1-5). Solomon had steeply increased income taxes to finance his program of public works projects, temple and palace building, and arms buildup.

Rehoboam asked advice from the older wise men of his father's administration. Their *counsel:* "Lower taxes and the people will do anything for you. Set an example of servanthood, and the people will be your servants."

IN A MULTITUDE OF COUNSELORS THERE IS SAFETY

Rehoboam also sought advice from his young friends who had graduated with him from Jerusalem University. They took a more short-range approach. Their *command:* "Speak harshly to the people; raise their taxes even higher. Show them who's boss from the start. If you give them an inch, they'll take a mile, so don't be a doormat."

The upshot of it all? Rehoboam ignored the wise counsel of his elders and split the kingdom in two! The ten Northern Tribes, led by Jeroboam, kept their tax money and set up a rival kingdom. Those who tried to collect taxes later for Rehoboam were killed. First Kings 12 gives the details on this story. For the next two centuries of the *CHASM* era these two Hebrew kingdoms were more enemies than allies.

Many Heads Make Life Work

It's interesting that Solomon tried to teach his son the value of wise counselors, both by principle and by practice. The Book of Proverbs was written by Solomon (Proverbs 1:1) to his son (Proverbs 2:1), most likely Rehoboam.

Use a Bible concordance to note the many references to wisdom in the book. The purpose of Proverbs is to increase the wisdom of all who read and heed it. Three times Solomon repeated the principle, "Many advisers make victory sure" (Proverbs 11:14; 15:22; 24:6).

Ask yourself—do you always follow the advice in God's Word, or from your parents? Your answer is probably "no way." But God is a good Teacher, and doesn't always simply *tell* us what's right. Sometimes He has to *show* us.

God communicates through the outcome of our choices. Rehoboam's heeding unwise counsel created a chasm in the kingdom that still exists. The ten Northern Tribes were scattered by Assyria and are still spread throughout the world. Not until the Lord returns to establish His kingdom and regather His people from the four corners of the earth will the Hebrew tribes again be united. (See Ezekiel 37:15-28.)

Wisdom's source is God, who freely shares His gifts with those who ask in reverent fear (Proverbs 1:7; James 1:5). Sometimes God's ideas are communicated through wise counselors. To us He has spoken clearly and firmly through His Son and in the Scriptures.

If you want knowledge, go to college or read a book. If you want wisdom, go to God and His Word. Follow David's example of regular meditation on the Scriptures (Psalm 119:97). For some practical help on getting more from the Bible, check out another Victor book, *Off the Shelf and Into Yourself*. For extra insight in facing life's decisions, consult older, wise counselors who are known for their godliness and spiritual growth.

What decisions are you facing today? Are you searching the Word and seeking the Source of wisdom? Are you consulting a multitude of older wise counselors? Are you asking God to reveal His will through people and events? Learn from Rehoboam's big mistake: there is safety in listening to wise counselors.

Separate Ways to Paydays

After Jeroboam's rebellion, a total of 18 more kings ruled over the ten Northern Tribes. Pagan worship centers were set up at Dan and Bethel, focusing on golden calves. It was the sin of Sinai all over again. Pilgrimages to Jerusalem were forbidden; Levites left the land in protest.

Did Rehoboam's wrong justify Jeroboam's rebellion?

Did Jeroboam "get away" with his treason against God? Negative on both scores! Read 1 Kings 14 to see how God personally collected from Jeroboam. The rest of the Books of Kings and Chronicles show how God collected His "due" for repeated spiritual robbery by Israel.

See what Israel reaped in the 209 years which came next. As a nation, they went in one direction—away from God. Their 19 kings had one thing in common: they were all bad in God's sight. The succession from father to son was broken nine times. There were two periods, totaling 20 years, when the throne was vacant. Only 7 of the 19 kings died a natural death. One was stricken by God; 2 died in battle; 1 committed suicide; 1 fell from an upper story; 6 were murdered; 1 died in captivity. Twelve ruled for twelve years or less; 1 ruled six months; another ruled just one month; and yet another held the throne only one week! Ten of the 19 kings were involved in major wars.

Finally Israel was captured by Assyria, and the people were scattered. The mixed race called Samaritans began here as Hebrews intermarried with pagans.

Judah's post-split history was somewhat more stable. In this Southern Kingdom, all 20 rulers were the descendants of King David. But only 8 kings of Judah received good evaluations from God. Read Kings and Chronicles for a record of reproofs and rewards meted out during each king's reign. Finally Babylon conquered Jerusalem and carried Judah into captivity.

Three Bible books record the CHASM era: 1 Kings 12—22, 2 Kings, and 2 Chronicles 10—36.

People Stirrers

God gave more-than-adequate warnings to both Hebrew kingdoms. A total of 30 prophets ministered

the message of Jehovah to the Jews during the divided kingdom period! Eight prophets from this period produced Bible books. The 22 others, including Elijah and Elisha, were too busy preaching to get any writing done. At the same time, three prophets served as foreign missionaries: Obadiah to Edom, and Jonah and Nahum to Assyria. God was continually offering His divine pardon to those who turned back to Him. For those who refused to repent, the results were clearly spelled out.

The prophets' sermons were loaded with double-barreled expectations: God's expectations for His people, and His people's expectations from Him. These spokesmen for God said as much or more about the failure of their own generations as they did about the future kingdom of God.

God expected fruit in His Old Testament vineyard. The prophets were raised up by the Heavenly Gardener to prune a knowledgeable nation back to its responsibilities. The prophets both comforted the afflicted and afflicted the comfortable who were at ease in Zion.

The prophets proclaimed the Maker's national recall program for Israel. The nation was not a credit to its Creator's character, as its people were not fulfilling His plan for their lives. Using clear words and pictures, the prophets tried to raise the fallen standard of God. They guaranteed that if the Jews didn't listen to God's warnings, they would be tossed out of their Promised Land. With such a "get tough" message, the prophets didn't exactly lead the popularity polls! In fact, the response of the general public wasn't much different from today's usual reaction: If the message gets too personal, persecute the preacher!

But the prophets' faith and faithfulness to the Lord only emphasized the faithlessness and unfaithfulness of the two Hebrew nations. True, in Judah there were brief periods of repentance and revival, usually led by a godly king who heeded his prophets with profit! But the general trend of the Israelites was a one-way street toward captivity and exile by foreign powers. Their suffering was their own fault because they did not listen to the prophets' strong warnings.

There is not one example in the Bible of judgment without warning. In every case, God not only warned but also offered pardon for repentance. He hasn't changed His ways. Is He trying to tell us anything through repeated correction in our lives? God would far rather have us voluntarily choose to cooperate with Him! But He will do whatever is necessary to encourage our obedience.

Part of the prophets' job was to *foretell* as well as *forthtell*. Foretelling the future was designed to encourage people to change, to give notice of God's judgment and to prove that judgment later on. Short-range predictions which came true in the prophet's lifetime verified the source of his sermons.

Long-range prophecies into the far future, sometimes not yet fulfilled, showed that God's discipline didn't mean divine displeasure. Chastening was always for correcting, not for casting off a people. Today God's original chosen people are spread around the world. But God has a glorious future in store for Israel. For God's Old Testament people too, the best is yet to come in Messiah's future kingdom. That kingdom is far more fully described in the Old Testament than in the New.

Prophets' Place

All 17 Old Testament Prophetic Books fall into the last three Old Testament eras (*CHASM, CAPTIVITIES,* and *CONSTRUCTION*). None of the Prophetic Books were written before the *CHASM* in the Hebrew kingdom, or after the Babylonian Captivity of the Jews.

The seven *CHASM* era prophets preached in four countries: two Hebrew countries (Israel and Judah) and two Gentile lands (Assyria and Edom). See the map on page 131. Lists of books in the same location are in chronological order.

Obadiah pronounced the doom of Edom, and Jonah proclaimed God's Word in Nineveh, the capital of Assyria. Amos and Hosea ministered in Israel.

The three *CHASM* prophets to Judah were Joel, Micah, and Isaiah, listed in the order they began their ministries, starting with the earliest.

What Did You Say?

Let's summarize the major message of the seven *CHASM* prophets, so when they greet us in glory, we'll not draw a total blank! They are listed in chronological order with their dates and place of work in parentheses. All dates are B.C. of course.

☐ **OBADIAH**—"Obliteration of Edom" (848-841 to Edom). Petra stands today as a silent testimony of the accuracy of Obadiah's prophecy against it. This red-rock city, capital of Edom, cut in the cliffs, is now only a center for jackals and vultures. What great sin did Edom commit so their place as well as their people should be cut off? They failed to help their brothers, the Jews, when the Jews were under attack. In fact, Edom aided the attackers. Comparable curses stand in Scripture today for those who are against the Jews.

☐ **JOEL**—"Judah's Judgment Day" (835-796 to Judah). A devastating locust plague in Joel's day became a fitting symbol of what invading human hordes

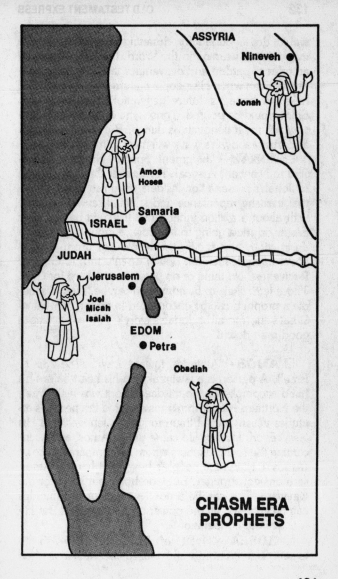

ASSYRIA

Nineveh ●

Jonah

Amos
Hosea

Samaria ●

ISRAEL

JUDAH

Jerusalem ●

Joel
Micah
Isaiah

EDOM

● Petra

Obadiah

**CHASM ERA
PROPHETS**

would do to Judah for deserting Jehovah. As with every divine warning in the Word, there was attached an offer of pardon and deliverance in return for repentance. Even when His people preferred judgment, God held out hope for future generations, on whom His Spirit would be poured. Those who insist on their own way will meet Jehovah as Judge. But those who turn and trust Jehovah's ways will meet Him as Saviour.

□ **JONAH**—"Judgment Spared Nineveh" (782-750 to Nineveh, Assyria). Far greater than the miracle of Jonah's preservation inside a great fish or sea mammal was the repentance and spiritual revival of a city with about a million inhabitants. It would be like your pastor or priest going to Moscow, announcing its soon destruction, and seeing the whole city (from the top government leaders on down) openly turn to God for forgiveness! No thing or no person is too hard for God. Those least likely to be converted can be. Even disobedient prophets can be encouraged to do the right thing! What's the moral of Jonah's story? You can't keep a good man down!

□ **AMOS**—"Attitudes toward Law" (782-739 to Israel). A person is a lawbreaker in his heart before his hand accomplishes the misdeed. So it was with Israel, the Northern Kingdom. Amos attacked the people's attitudes which caused them to ignore Jehovah and His laws. Every level of life came under Amos' attack, including the social climbers whom he compared to cows (Amos 4:1). As the people's hearts got harder, Amos' sermons got stronger. But God holds out hope for the wayward. This can be a positive note for us: attitudes can be changed by the power of the Almighty! But He requires our cooperation.

□ **HOSEA**—"Heart of Holiness" (755-715 to Israel). Deuteronomy and Hosea are similar in their dual emphasis on God's love and holiness. Only God can be awesomely perfect and absolutely loving at the same time. His holiness doesn't override what is best for His creatures; nor does His love approve of lack of perfection. God's solution is to let love offer repentant rebels a gift of righteousness. But the key is repentance. Hosea called Israel to return to her God, using God's constant love as their motivation. The prophet even married (or remarried) a harlot named Gomer to dramatically show that God desired reunion with estranged Israel. God's love should prompt us to turn from our independence and return to a relationship of dependence on our Maker as our Saviour.

☐ **MICAH**—"Morality in Society" (740-690 to Judah). Micah was Judah's counterpart to Israel's Amos. Every segment of society was found short on morality. The final remedy would be a whole new society, governed by the Messiah Himself. God would begin this interrupted process with a Babe in Bethlehem (Micah 5:2) who would first be Saviour and later Sovereign. Micah's message holds true for us today. We must become members of God's spiritual kingdom now, if we're to participate in His earthly kingdom later.

☐ **ISAIAH**—"Israel's Suffering, Glory" (740-680 to Judah). The 66 chapters of Isaiah form a miniature Bible, dividing into 39 about Israel's past suffering and 27 about her future glory in Messiah's millennial kingdom. There is a clear correspondence in size and subject matter to Isaiah's two "testaments." The second segment (Isaiah 40—66) divides into three parts of 9 chapters each, marked by a closing doxology. The center chapter of the center section is chapter 53, about the cross of Christ! As with Messiah and Israel, so with us—suffering in the present can't be compared to the glory that will follow for the children of God (see Romans 8:18).

What's the Score?

During the *CHASM* era, the people of Nineveh ended up with the best scores. Though they entered this historical era as the cruelest country, they repented of their sins after hearing Jonah's sermons. They heeded the wise counsel of God's prophet and were spared the terrible end they deserved. Unfortunately, Nineveh's overthrow was just delayed for about 150 years, as you'll see from Nahum's ministry in the next chapter.

Nineteen kings of Israel, during a span of 208 years, managed to completely disregard the messages of Amos and Hosea. Hence, the Northern Kingdom was the first of the two Hebrew nations to enter the *CAP-TIVITIES* era. Israel flunked the wise counselor test.

Judah, the Southern Kingdom, received mixed ratings. Because six of her twelve kings listened to God's prophets during the *CHASM* era, Judah was allowed to exist another 136 years after Israel was scattered by Assyria.

If the history books of eternity could be opened to the chapter on your life, what would be your rating for listening to and heeding wise counsel? Give yourself an overall average between 0 (for never seeking nor heeding wise counselors) and 20 (for always seeking and heeding wise counselors).

Perhaps by starting today, there will still be time to raise your rating before the last chapter in your personal history is written.

12

TIME FOR A REST

CAPTIVITIES Era (2 Kings 17—25; 2 Chronicles 29—36)

A total of seven prophetic books were produced during the *CAPTIVITIES* era, the same number as during the *CHASM* era. Again, prophets ministered to two Gentile nations (Nahum to Assyria and Daniel to Babylon) and to two Jewish groups. Zephaniah, Jeremiah, Habakkuk, and Lamentations were directed toward Jews in Judah and Ezekiel spoke to Jews in Babylon.

In chapter 11, we described Israel's rebellion against Rehoboam and Jehovah. The capstone to this rebellion was the Assyrian conquest which scattered the ten Northern Tribes in 722 B.C. (2 Kings 17). See the *CAPTIVITIES* era map on page 136.

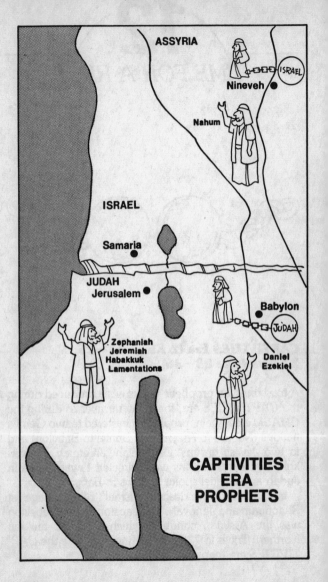

ASSYRIA

ISRAEL

Nineveh ●

Nahum

ISRAEL

Samaria ●

JUDAH
Jerusalem ●

Babylon

JUDAH

Zephaniah
Jeremiah
Habakkuk
Lamentations

Daniel
Ezekiel

**CAPTIVITIES
ERA
PROPHETS**

Assyria (with headquarters at Nineveh) was one of the cruelest robber nations. Assyrian warriors would cut off captives' hands, feet, or noses, and make a great pile of skulls. Seeing a fellow Israelite staked to the ground and flayed alive certainly put the fear of the Assyrians into one's soul as well as a strong desire to obey their every order. Israel's sin paid high wages!

The first Hebrew prophet to proclaim God's Word in Nineveh was Jonah. The last three letters of *Jonah* begin to spell the name of the other prophet to Assyria, *Nahum*.

☐ **NAHUM**—"Nineveh's Soon Judgment" (661-612 to Nineveh, Assyria). Revivals are usually only temporary, and Nineveh's under Jonah (during the *CHASM* era) was no exception. Nearly a century later the Assyrian cup of evil was again overflowing, and their overthrow was about to take place. Nahum even predicted how the fortress-like city—surrounded by moats, walls, and high towers—would be taken by a combination of fire and flood (Nahum 1:8; 3:15). The people of Nineveh had not learned that human defenses, no matter how strong, are no help in God's day of reckoning. The only sure security is to have a close relationship with the Eternal One.

Time to Shape Up

It's no surprise that Israel should be the first of the two Hebrew nations to be conquered. After all, they had 19 straight losers for kings! Judah scored higher with 8 good rulers out of 20 between Solomon and the Babylonian Captivity.

The *CAPTIVITIES* era began with Assyria scattering Israel in 722 B.C. and ended with the first Jewish exiles returning from Babylon in 536 B.C. After Israel's fall,

Judah was allowed 136 additional years to shape up before they were shipped out. During this period Judah had eight more kings, only two of whom were good in God's eyes—Hezekiah and Josiah. There were also three more prophets—Zephaniah, Jeremiah, and Habakkuk. (Keep in mind that all dates in this chapter are B.C.)

☐ **ZEPHANIAH**—"Zion's Remnant Saved" (630 to Judah). In every age, only a faithful few follow God. But at least there are always some alive in the line of faith. On the eve of Judah's Captivity by Babylon, Zephaniah encouraged these faithful few. Even though Judah was about to be judged, a remnant of them would one day return to Zion (another name for Jerusalem). Zephaniah's words must have been uplifting during the 70-year Captivity: "The Lord your God is with you, He is mighty to save. He will take great delight in you, He will quiet you with His love, He will rejoice over you with singing" (Zephaniah 3:17).

Zephaniah affirmed that God was still identified with His people. He was still mighty; He would save them in due time. God was settled in His love for His people. In fact, He was still rejoicing over them!

Do you need something to pick you up when you're down, or to start your day off on the right spiritual step? Write the words of Zephaniah 3:17 in large letters on a card and place it where you'll see it first thing in the morning. Then read it back to God, thanking Him for each truth in it.

☐ **JEREMIAH**—"Judah's Exile, Return" (627-586 to Judah). Jeremiah's faithfulness in proclaiming Judah's coming 70-year Babylonian bondage put this prophet at the bottom of the popularity polls. Before Nebuchadnezzar came, Jeremiah urged his people to cooperate with the conquerors. Afterward (Jeremiah 30—52), he encouraged the captives to settle down

SCENES FROM JEREMIAH

and make the most of their 70 years. He told them they
would come back—but not any sooner than foretold.
Divine discipline is strict but designed for good in the
lives of all of God's people—then and now.

How many of the symbols on page 139 from Jeremiah's life and lips can you identify?

☐ **HABAKKUK**—"Humanity and Sovereignty"
(610-599 to Judah). As Habakkuk saw sin rampaging
in Judah, he questioned God's seeming inactivity.
Sound modern? When God showed His prophet that
the Babylonians were being prepared for a Jewish judgment, Habakkuk had another question. How can a
holy God use unholy tools to do His work in the world?
God answered that the invaders would be judged for
their own sins in due time. God's use of a nation doesn't
sanctify them or excuse them. To achieve His ends,
God can and will use whomever He wishes, but everyone is still held responsible for his own choices. God
does respond to honest doubts; Habakkuk was never
scolded on that score. But it's also dangerous to put
God in any box and think that He can't work in a different way than we expect. Though God never violates
His Word or His character, He does things in His own
ways.

Divine Collections

King Nebuchadnezzar of Babylon conquered Judah,
the Southern Kingdom, three times. In 606 he subdued
the people and took captive some of the leadership (including Daniel). In 597 he invaded again and took
more of the people into exile (including the Prophet
Ezekiel). After further uprisings by the Jews, Nebuchadnezzar finally leveled Jerusalem and the temple.

The Babylonian Captivity lasted 70 years on two

counts. From 606 (first exile of Jews to Babylon) to 536 (first return of Jews to Judah from Babylon) marks the political captivity. From 586 (temple destruction) to 516 (temple reconstruction) marks the religious captivity.

Why did God pick the number 70 as the number of years for Judah's Babylonian Captivity? Was it only to fulfill Jeremiah's prophecy? (Jeremiah 25:11-12; 29:10) Which sin of Judah called for a 70-year penalty to match the crime? The answer is found in one of the less-familiar sections of Scripture—2 Chronicles 36:20-21. God determined the 70 years by the number of Sabbaths His people had robbed during the 820 years they lived in the Promised Land!

Remember, God had commanded them to let the land and people rest 1 day out of each week, 1 year out of each 7, and an extra year every 49 years (see Leviticus 23—26). For generations it seemed they were getting away with not doing this. I wonder how the one who started this chain of cheating must have felt. Did he wonder if a thunderbolt might strike him dead? Did he remember the Sabbath-breaker stoned to death in Moses' day? (Numbers 15:32-36)

I can still remember planning a "perfect" crime as a grade-schooler. With my folks away, no one would know I rode my two-wheeler on a forbidden highway to an off-limits swimming hole with the gang. Though I was too nervous the whole time to really enjoy myself, I was relieved to get home before Mom and Dad. But there was only one problem, which I became aware of later by a belt on my bottom—my older brother had been watching.

As the Hebrews' Sabbath-breaking became a nation-wide habit, heaven seemed silent. But the Hebrews made the same mistake as modern-day scoffers. They confused God's patience for a slackness in keeping His Word (2 Peter 3:9). God is patient because He is not willing that any should perish, but that all should come back to Him. Through the years of reproofs by prophets and circumstances, God's goodness was designed to lead His people to repentance (Romans 2:4).

God was keeping an accurate record all the time. When Judah accumulated a debt of 70 years' worth of Sabbaths, God came to collect!

Have you ever felt smug and self-satisfied for "getting away" with something, feeling no one who matters knows about it? Be reminded from 2 Kings and 2 Chronicles that God sees everything and keeps perfect records. Any seeming interval of freedom is His being patient, to allow you time for self-judgment and correction. But God's long-suffering has limits. Eventually He will collect whatever is still due Him.

Suffering While Serving

Satan would mislead us to believe that all of our suffering results from our sins. It is true that the basis for all suffering can be traced back to man's original sin in the Garden. It's true that there will be no suffering when sin` is forever banished from the new heavens and new earth. But it is not true that all our suffering is due to our personal sins. Note how Jesus corrected His mistaken disciples on this issue (John 9:1-3).

The Lord also corrected Job's miserable visitors who merely added to his sufferings by insisting that he repent of whatever terrible sin was in his life (Job 42). Often those who serve God faithfully endure sufferings that are not directly related to any personal failures.

During the time of the Babylonian bondage, God faithfully encouraged His people. God kept reaffirming His love during this period of divine discipline. Three prophets ministered during the 70 years of the Babylo-

SCENES FROM DANIEL

MENE.
MENE.
TEKEL.
PARSIN

nian Captivity. Jeremiah was left behind to witness the destruction of Jerusalem, minister to the small remnant of Jews, and finally to flee with them to Egypt. (Refer again to the *CAPTIVITIES* era map on page 136.)

In Babylon God had His witness both in the palace and among the Jewish populace. Can you recall which man was specially gifted to minister to royalty? The one who purposed in his heart that he would not defile himself with the king's unkosher diet? It was Daniel, who was captured with the first group of exiles.

□ **DANIEL**—"Days of Gentiles" (606-534 to Babylon). While Ezekiel was encouraging the exiles with what they could expect regarding the temple, Daniel was revealing God's program for the Gentiles to the princely powers of Babylon. Daniel issued a series of specific prophecies about four great world powers— Babylon, Medo-Persia, Greece, and Rome. The stories of Daniel's eventful life have probably been spun more than any other prophets', except perhaps Jonah's. How much can you recall of them by studying the symbols on page 143?

□ **EZEKIEL**—"Expectations for Temple" (593-571 to Babylon). Similar to Isaiah and Jeremiah, Ezekiel first wrote of Judah's discipline, then her delight, devoting 24 chapters to each. But the core around which Ezekiel wound his writing was the temple in Jerusalem. As the Holy Spirit departed from the defiled temple, the people were forced to depart from their land. Ezekiel's message of hope included the future rebuilding of the temple on a grand scale.

Ezekiel was a master communicator, using more audio and visual aids than any other prophet except Jesus. Some of his "sight-and-sense sermons" have been captured in symbols on page 145. How many can you describe?

□ **LAMENTATIONS**—"Lament Over Jerusa-

SCENES FROM EZEKIEL

lem." Jeremiah is the only prophet to produce two books. Instead of calling his second book "Jeremiah, Jr.," he called it Lamentations, making it the only Old Testament prophetic book that was not named for its human author. This eyewitness account by Jeremiah of the Babylonians' siege and sack of Jerusalem is one of the saddest stories of Scripture. Lamentations was composed as an acrostic and is still read and recited by orthodox Jewry at the Jerusalem wailing wall, below the old temple mount.

To recall the prophetic books of the Babylonian Captivity, remember there were three prophets who were "LED" into captivity. Since the Captivity was really a step backward for the Jews to pay for their robbed Sabbaths, read the acrostic backwards to recall *D*aniel, *E*zekiel, and *L*amentations in chronological order.

Good Guys Do Too

Though Daniel, Ezekiel, and Jeremiah were outwardly quite different in their ministries to princes and people, each had to endure much suffering in their faithful service to the Lord. Daniel is most famous for his miraculous delivery from the lions' den, but he also had to endure the first siege and conquest of Jerusalem. He was taken captive about 900 miles from home, lived under a death penalty for a time with the other wise men, and once spent weeks in mourning after a heavy vision.

Ezekiel was greatly persecuted by his fellow Jews for bringing them an unpopular message. He also had to lie on one side for 430 days, was shaved bald, and wasn't allowed to mourn when his beloved wife died.

Jeremiah so mourned over the suffering of his people that he was called "the weeping prophet." At one point he was confined to a mud-filled pit, and when he was finally pulled out, he was imprisoned in chains.

For each of these faithful servants, suffering for well-doing was a part of their calling. The Apostle Peter, in a chapter about suffering, reminded us that the Lord Jesus has left us an example, that we should follow in His steps (1 Peter 4). Paul stated that we are called unto the sufferings of Christ, anticipating those glories that will follow (Romans 8). The account of Job reminds us that the reason for some suffering is the glory of God—for certain good purposes He has for His creation which can't be accomplished any other way.

Suffering for well-doing is definitely not to be sought. If suffering *is* sent as a part of our service to God, how is it worthwhile? Read Jesus' answer (Matthew 5:11-12) and Paul's answers (Romans 8:18; 2 Corinthians 12:1-10).

Does suffering result in rewards? Ask Daniel, Ezekiel, or Jeremiah when you meet them in glory. I know what their answer will be!

13

THREE TRIPS BACK

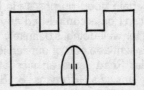

CONSTRUCTION Era (Ezra—Esther)

The strange handwriting on the wall was the beginning of the end of the Babylonian Captivity.

Babylon was a beautiful capital city, complete with gorgeous hanging gardens, peerless palaces, and streamlined streets. Having conquered most of the known world, the people of Babylon were happy to eat, drink, and make merry. On this particular night in 536 B.C. the feast of King Belshazzar was *the* place to be. Anybody who was anybody was there. Suddenly the din of the orgy was drowned in silence as a heavenly hand appeared and wrote on the ballroom wall: "Mene, Mene, Tekel, Parsin."

The Prophet Daniel was the only man wise enough

to interpret the four foreign words. His translation earned him a promotion to the number three spot in the kingdom. But that very night King Belshazzar was killed and Babylon conquered by the Persians—just as the handwriting predicted. The words meant, "God has numbered the days of your reign and brought it to an end. You have been weighed on the scales and found wanting. Your kingdom is divided and given to the Persians." You can read the full account of these events in Daniel 5.

Too Hot to Handle

During the Babylonian Captivity, Persia conquered Babylonia to become the new world power. But unlike the Jews during the *CYCLES* era of the Judges, the Persians *did* learn something from history. They thought of past peoples who persecuted Hebrews and the terrible results. When Egypt would not let the Israelites go free, they suffered from ten punishing plagues. Later Egypt was conquered by Assyria.

Assyria conquered and scattered Israel, but later Assyria was conquered by Babylonia. Babylonia destroyed Jerusalem and took most of the surviving Jewish populace into exile. Their power only lasted until the Persians came and conquered.

Much like the Philistines in the days of Eli who found the ark of God too hot to handle, the Persians realized the consequences of keeping Jews in bondage in Babylon just weren't worth it.

So Cyrus, King of Persia, freed the Jews who were in Babylon to return to Judah. The year was 536 B.C., exactly 70 years after the first deportation from Judah in 606.

The Way Back

The Books of Ezra and Nehemiah record three groups of Jews coming out of the Babylonian Captivity, returning back to Jerusalem in Judah. These journeys probably followed the fertile crescent, instead of crossing the Arabian Desert. See the *CONSTRUCTION* era map on page 151.

Esther became queen of Persia after the first group returned from bondage in Babylon and before the second arrived. This closing Old Testament *CONSTRUCTION* period, when the Jews returned to rebuild the city of Jerusalem, can be summarized thus:

☐ 536 B.C.—Zerubbabel leads some Jews back to Jerusalem to rebuild the temple (Ezra 1—6). King

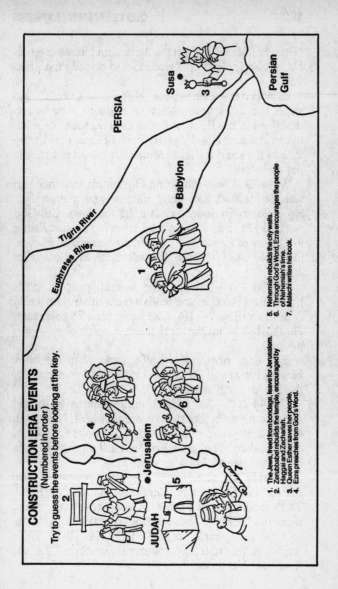

CONSTRUCTION ERA EVENTS
(Numbered in order)

Try to guess the events before looking at the key.

PERSIA

Susa

Babylon

Persian Gulf

Tigris River

Euphrates River

JUDAH

Jerusalem

1. The Jews, freed from bondage, leave for Jerusalem.
2. Zerubbabel rebuilds the temple, encouraged by Haggai and Zechariah.
3. Queen Esther saves her people.
4. Ezra preaches from God's Word.
5. Nehemiah rebuilds the city walls.
6. Through God's Word, Ezra encourages the people of Nehemiah's time.
7. Malachi writes his book.

Nebuchadnezzar had left the Jerusalem temple in a *rubble*, so God raised up *Zerubba*bel to remedy the situation.

☐ 478 B.C.—Esther wins "Miss Persia Contest" and saves the Jews from a decree of death. The events described in the Book of Esther actually took place between chapters 6 and 7 of the Book of Ezra. Line up the 2 *E*s of *E*zra and *E*sther to remember these books are in the same era.

While God was rebuilding His temple in Jerusalem with Zerubbabel, Satan and Haman were masterminding a plot in Shushan, Persia to kill the Jews. But God rescued His chosen people by elevating Jewess Esther to Queen of Persia in a masterful counterplot! Hence, the three-word title for Esther's book is "Escape of Jews."

☐ 458 B.C.—Ezra brings a second group of exiles home from Babylon and leads a great spiritual revival in Jerusalem (Ezra 7—10). Ezra came back 78 years after Zerubbabel to inspire and teach a spiritually sagging people.

Ezra does not appear until chapter 7 in the book bearing his name; Zerubbabel is the lead character for the first six chapters.

☐ 444 B.C.—Nehemiah's group returns to rebuild Jerusalem's walls. Fourteen years after Ezra, Nehemiah led the third group home, to rebuild the walls of the city of Jerusalem. The same Ezra was still on duty to help revive the people in Nehemiah's time.

Because the stones of Jerusalem became so dirty during the Babylonian Captivity, the *CONSTRUCTION* workers used a powerful cleanser with the brand name of "ZEEN." These four letters remind us of the four major people during the *CONSTRUCTION* period, in the order they appeared: *Z*erubbabel, *E*sther, *E*zra, and *N*ehemiah.

The Balanced Life

It's interesting that both records of restoration, Ezra and Nehemiah, divide roughly in half, with the first half emphasizing physical activity and the second half focusing on spiritual activity. Ezra has two returns while Nehemiah has two buildings. Ezra (1—6) sees the temple rebuilt; Nehemiah (1—6) sees the walls rebuilt. In Ezra (7—10) the people are revived; in Nehemiah (7—13) the people are rebuilt spiritually.

Ezra has been captioned "Erection of Temple" and Nehemiah, "New City Walls."

The "balanced life" in these twin books is a balance between physical and spiritual activity. Even as physical activity is necessary for a healthy life, so spiritual activity is necessary for your soul and spirit, to develop your

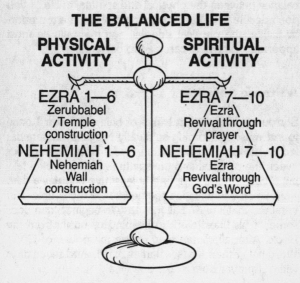

THE BALANCED LIFE
PHYSICAL ACTIVITY
SPIRITUAL ACTIVITY

EZRA 1—6
Zerubbabel
Temple
construction

EZRA 7—10
Ezra
Revival through
prayer

NEHEMIAH 1—6
Nehemiah
Wall
construction

NEHEMIAH 7—10
Ezra
Revival through
God's Word

love and growth toward God.

For example, as you think about the week just passed, I'm sure you can recall a number of physical things you did. Some were necessary for your survival, others weren't. Now stop and think about how much time you've taken out of the last seven days (a total of 168 hours) to develop your spiritual life—walk with the Lord through His Word. Have you read some Scripture this week during some prime time? What about studying, memorizing, thinking about, or applying some portion of your Father's Word? Has prayer been a part of this passing week? If so, did it go beyond petition to praise and adoration of the Almighty One? How many cups of cold water have you carried in concern for others? Was the first part of your income set aside for Him?

Ezra and Nehemiah teach us to look for a blessed balance between the physical and spiritual in life. If you don't decide to develop your spiritual life as a top priority in life, the physical side will automatically be most important. Busyness can lead to barrenness!

A Strong Solution

Surrounded by the pressures of being a pastor I once found myself becoming spiritually irregular. A seminar led by Bill Gothard helped me find a better balance between the physical and the spiritual. He suggested taking a vow to read Scripture at least five minutes a day.

At first the whole idea seemed a little too simple. But I realized that it wasn't all that easy to begin. Satan does some of his finest work in keeping us busily from the Book. After all, Satan may realize the power of God's Word better than we (see James 2:19). And seven days without prayer does make one weak!

Once I made the vow, I found it strong enough to cause me to have a devotional time daily for the twelve years since. Some days I've only read for the promised five minutes, but at least it was something!

God takes vows seriously. Read Ecclesiastes 5:1-7 before ever making one. The Lord also takes the responsibility to remind us daily of such a vow. I know from the nights I have been in bed, just getting cozily warm, when in my head the words pound, "My vow! My vow!" To go to sleep over that strong reminder would be clear, defiant sin.

The Last Three Preachers

The final three Old Testament prophets are Haggai, Zechariah, and Malachi. Here's an overview of these last, but not least, Old Testament prophets:

☐ **HAGGAI**—"House of God" (520 B.C.). Zerubbabel had the encouragement of both Haggai (pronounced HAG-eye in two syllables only) and Zechariah (pronounced with a short "e") in rebuilding the temple in Jerusalem after the Babylonian Captivity. Haggai's preaching prodded the people to get to work building God's house instead of their own home improvement projects. Matthew 6:33 could be written to summarize Haggai's sermon notes, "But seek first His kingdom and His righteousness, and all these things will be given to you as well." Putting God first has been proper in every age. When we do, He assumes the responsibility to meet all our needs.

☐ **ZECHARIAH**—"Zion's Remnant Saved" (520-518 B.C.). Zechariah took a long-range look down the corridor of time to the two comings of the Messiah, with emphasis on the Second Coming. During the physical work of rebuilding the temple on Mount Zion, God was also concerned about a spiritual work in the hearts of His people.

Are you ever discouraged because your life seems too unimportant compared with your dreams or memories? Does Satan remind you of your failures, telling you God can't use you now? Let Zechariah encourage you that God can do greater things in and through you than you have ever imagined! (See Jeremiah 33:3.) Some of God's greatest works have been done through people who had failed Him miserably—people like Jonah and David. There's great hope, if your heart is set on God's will and glory!

☐ **MALACHI**—"Messenger Before Messiah" (435-424 B.C.). Malachi drew the curtain on prophetic performance in the Old Testament. But he rearranged the stage for the next act before he left. The Star of the show was yet to come. And that scene would open with one who would come as a forerunner in the spirit and power of Elijah, a prophecy that John the Baptist would fulfill.

Malachi also described the spiritual condition of God's chosen people after more than 2,000 years of revelation, rescue, and revival since Abraham's day. The people were no longer trusting, and held God at a distance. A similar spirit was still present when the Messiah appeared personally.

It's sad that the Old Testament, which began with creation of the earth by God, had to end with a curse on that earth by Him. You'll find that curse in the Old Testament's last verse (Malachi 4:6). Notice how this contrasts with the last verse of the New Testament, which ends with a blessing!

Malachi closes the Old Testament looking forward to the coming Messiah. If you'd read the Bible as a single book from beginning to end, with no prior knowledge of what's in it, you would realize the story can't end at

Malachi. The Hero hasn't come yet. The challenge against God and good is still too strong. The promise of a perfect Prophet, perfect Priest, and perfect King had not been fulfilled. It was up to one Person to meet all three of these requirements.

Tying It Together

After Malachi there were 400 years of prophetless (and mostly profitless) existence for God's Old Testament people. Then the New Testament opened with the announcement and arrival of the long-awaited Hero—Jesus Christ!

What a story developed between Moses and Malachi! But are our personal stories much different? Or do they

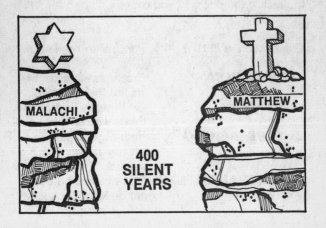

also prove that some things (such as God and people) don't change? God is still showing Himself faithful. But are we faithful in return? He still does miracles; do we still murmur soon afterward? God still reveals Himself in Scripture; but do we often refuse to hear or read and heed?

We can learn the hard way or the easy way. The easy way is to profit from those who had to learn the hard way. Really, the choice is ours. But one thing is certain: we *will* learn, one way or the other!

It's dangerous to view the Old Testament history, experience, and prophecy as simply facts and information. Instead, Old Testament lessons should inspire us to action. Or we might feel too overwhelmed with all that should be done to practice these principles in our lives. But we can't let all that we *can't* do keep us from at least one thing we *can* do—*today!* Because I can't do *everything*, I won't refuse to do *something*.

Look at the following list of Old Testament themes, and pick one principle to work on especially. Ask the Lord to help you write down two or three action steps to practice the principle you chose.

Old Testament Era	Principle to Apply
1. **CREATION**	Creatures are accountable to their Creator.
2. **CLAN**	God usually begins new things with people.
3. **CONFINEMENT**	Both physical and spiritual redemption are needed.
4. **COMMANDMENTS**	God's commandments are designed for successful living.

5. **CAMPING**	God tests what He has taught.
6. **COVENANT**	Loving God is a choice to be made.
7. **CONQUEST**	Success in life requires cooperation with God.
8. **CYCLES**	Those who ignore the past are condemned to repeat it.
9. **CROWNS**	A good start doesn't guarantee a good end.
10. **CHASM**	There is safety in heeding the advice of wise counselors.
11. **CAPTIVITIES**	No one can successfully rob God.
12. **CONSTRUCTION**	Physical activity must be balanced with spiritual.